Activity Book

Science

PEARSON
Scott Foresman

Editorial Offices: Glenview, Illinois • Parsippany, New Jersey • New York, New York
Sales Offices: Needham, Massachusetts • Duluth, Georgia • Glenview, Illinois
Coppell, Texas • Sacramento, California • Mesa, Arizona

www.sfsuccessnet.com

Series Authors

Dr. Timothy Cooney
Professor of Earth Science and Science Education
University of Northern Iowa (UNI)
Cedar Falls, Iowa

Dr. Jim Cummins
Professor
Department of Curriculum, Teaching, and Learning
The University of Toronto
Toronto, Canada

Dr. James Flood
Distinguished Professor of Literacy and Language
School of Teacher Education
San Diego State University
San Diego, California

Barbara Kay Foots, M.Ed.
Science Education Consultant
Houston, Texas

Dr. M. Jenice Goldston
Associate Professor of Science Education
Department of Elementary Education Programs
University of Alabama
Tuscaloosa, Alabama

Dr. Shirley Gholston Key
Associate Professor of Science Education
Instruction and Curriculum Leadership Department
College of Education
University of Memphis
Memphis, Tennessee

Dr. Diane Lapp
Distinguished Professor of Reading and Language Arts in Teacher Education
San Diego State University
San Diego, California

Sheryl A. Mercier
Classroom Teacher
Dunlap Elementary School
Dunlap, California

Dr. Karen L. Ostlund
UTeach, College of Natural Sciences
The University of Texas at Austin
Austin, Texas

Dr. Nancy Romance
Professor of Science Education & Principal Investigator
NSF/IERI Science IDEAS Project
Charles E. Schmidt College of Science
Florida Atlantic University
Boca Raton, Florida

Dr. William Tate
Chair and Professor of Education and Applied Statistics
Department of Education
Washington University
St. Louis, Missouri

Dr. Kathryn C. Thornton
Professor
School of Engineering and Applied Science
University of Virginia
Charlottesville, Virginia

Dr. Leon Ukens
Professor of Science Education
Department of Physics, Astronomy, and Geosciences
Towson University
Towson, Maryland

Steve Weinberg
Consultant
Connecticut Center for Advanced Technology
East Hartford, Connecticut

Consulting Author

Dr. Michael P. Klentschy
Superintendent
El Centro Elementary School District
El Centro, California

ISBN: 0-328-12625-X

3 4 5 6 7 8 9 10 V084 13 12 11 10 09 08 07 06

Process Skill Activities

Activity Record Sheets

Unit A
Life Science

Unit B
Earth Science

Unit C
Physical Science

Unit D
Space and Technology

Science Safety

Scientists know they must work safely when doing experiments. You need to be careful when doing science activities too. Follow these safety rules.

- Read the activity carefully before you start to do it.
- Listen to the teacher's instructions. Ask questions about things you do not understand.
- Wear safety goggles when needed.
- Keep your work place neat and clean. Clean up spills right away.
- Never taste or smell substances unless directed to do so by your teacher.
- Handle sharp items and other equipment carefully.
- Use chemicals carefully.
- Help keep plants and animals you use safe.
- Tell your teacher if you have an accident or you see something that looks unsafe.
- Put materials away when you finish an inquiry.
- Dispose of chemicals properly.
- Wash your hands well when you are finished.

Name ___________________________

Practice Observing

Observe means to use your senses to learn about objects, events, or living things. You can observe properties, characteristics, differences, similarities, and changes. In this activity, you will observe the properties of four objects.

Materials

penny
rubber band
wood block
sandpaper

What to Do

1. Observe the weight, texture, appearance, and flexibility of the four objects.
2. Record your observations in the chart.

Object	Texture	Appearance	Flexibility		Weight	
	Is the object rough or smooth?	Is the object dull or shiny?	Does the object bend?	Does the object stretch?	The object is heavier than a ______.	The object is lighter than a ______.
penny						
rubber band						
wood block						
sand-paper						

Name ______________________________________

Explain Your Results

1. How many of the objects had a shiny appearance? How many were dull?

____

2. What else can you observe about the objects? Name two properties you can observe that are not in the chart.

____

____

____

Name ____________________

Practice Communicating

Communicating means sharing information using words, pictures, charts, and graphs. In this activity, you will communicate what happens when you try to clean some pennies.

Materials

2 plastic cups	plastic teaspoon
vinegar	4 pennies
water	paper towel
salt	clock or watch

What to Do

1. Fill one plastic cup halfway with vinegar. Add 1 teaspoon salt. Stir until the salt dissolves.
2. Fill the other plastic cup halfway with water.
3. Look at the pennies. How would you describe their color? Are they shiny or dull? Clean or dirty? Write a description of their appearance in the chart.
4. Use the spoon to add the pennies to the vinegar and salt mixture. Make sure the pennies do not cover each other.
5. Wait 5 minutes. Do you observe any changes in the appearance of the pennies? Record your observations in the chart.
6. Use the spoon to remove 2 pennies and lay them on the paper towel to dry. Do not rinse them off.
7. Remove the other 2 pennies and rinse them off in the water. Then lay them on the paper towel to dry.
8. Observe the appearance of the pennies that were rinsed in water and the pennies that weren't rinsed. Record your observations in the chart.

Name ______________________________

Before and After Dipping Pennies in Vinegar			
	Color	Shine	Overall Cleanliness
Before being placed in the vinegar			
After 5 minutes in the vinegar			

After Drying			
	Color	Shine	Overall Cleanliness
Rinsed in water			
Not rinsed in water			

Explain Your Results

1. *Compare* means to describe similarities between objects. *Contrast* means to describe differences between objects. Compare and contrast the appearances of the pennies that were rinsed with the pennies that weren't rinsed.

____

____

____

2. Suppose you wanted to clean a whole jar of pennies. Describe the best way to clean a jar of pennies.

____

____

Name ______________________

Practice Estimating and Measuring

Estimating and measuring means making a reasonable calculation about a quantity and then finding out if your calculation is accurate. In this activity, you will estimate how many field mice are living in a cornfield.

Materials

index card (3 in. × 5 in.)
scissors
tape
paper grid with 3 rows and 3 columns of 1 in. squares (to represent a cornfield)
2 teaspoons of lentils (to represent field mice)

What to Do

1. Fold the index card into 4 equal pieces and then cut along the folds. Tape the pieces together to form a square barrier. Place the square barrier around the grid.
2. Place 2 teaspoons of lentils in the middle of the grid. The grid represents sections of a cornfield where field mice live.
3. Hold the barrier in place and shake the grid. Make sure the lentils are spread evenly. The lentils represent field mice.
4. Remove the barrier. Count the field mice in 1 square. Write down the number.
   Field mice in square 1: ____
5. Count the field mice in another square. Write down the the number.
   Field mice in square 2: ____
6. Add the numbers of field mice you counted to find the total number of mice in the two squares.

	+		=	
field mice in first square		field mice in second square		total field mice in 2 squares

Name ___________________________________

7 Divide the sum by 2 to find the average number of field mice in each square.

	÷	2	=	
total field mice in 2 squares		number of squares counted		average number of field mice per square

8 Now you must multiply the average number of field mice in each square by the total number of squares, 9, to find the estimated number of field mice in the whole cornfield.

	×	9	=	
average number of field mice per square		total number of squares		estimated number of field mice living in the cornfield

9 Count all the lentils on the grid to find the actual number of field mice living in the cornfield.

Actual number of field mice in the cornfield: ____

Explain Your Results

1. How close was your estimate to the exact number of field mice?

____

2. Imagine that a beekeeper needed to find the number of bees in a hive. Why might the beekeeper choose to estimate the number of bees instead of counting them?

____

____

3. Name another situation in which you would estimate a quantity instead of counting.

____

Name ______________________________

Practice Collecting Data

Collecting data means gathering information about observations and measurements in an organized way, such as charts, graphs, and diagrams. When data is organized, you can look for patterns that will help you understand what you observed. In this activity, you will find what percentage of your classroom population has certain physical traits.

What to Do

1. Complete column 1 of the *Traits Tally* chart on page 8.
2. Tally your group's results in column 2 of the *Traits Tally* sheet.
3. Share your results with other groups in the class until you have tallied information from everyone in the class on your *Traits Tally* sheet.
4. Find your total classroom population by counting how many students are in the class.
5. Divide the class tally for each trait by the classroom population to find the percentage of students who have each trait.

Traits Tally

	My Traits Mark an X if you have the trait.	**Class Tally** Tally the results of all the students in the class for each trait.	**% Students with the Trait** Divide the Class Tally by the total population of the class.
Right-handed			
Left-handed			
Curly hair			
Straight hair			
Freckles			
No freckles			
Dark hair			
Blond hair			
Red hair			
Dimples			
No dimples			

Total Classroom Population: ______________________________

Explain Your Results

1. How did you organize your data?

____

____

____

2. List 3 patterns you found in your data.

____

____

____

Name ________________________________

Practice Classifying

Classify means to arrange or group objects according to their common properties. In this activity, you will observe the characteristics of six animals and classify the animals by their physical characteristics.

Materials

pictures of animals

A. Cottontail Rabbit

B. Bald Eagle

C. Black Bear

D. Mountain Lion

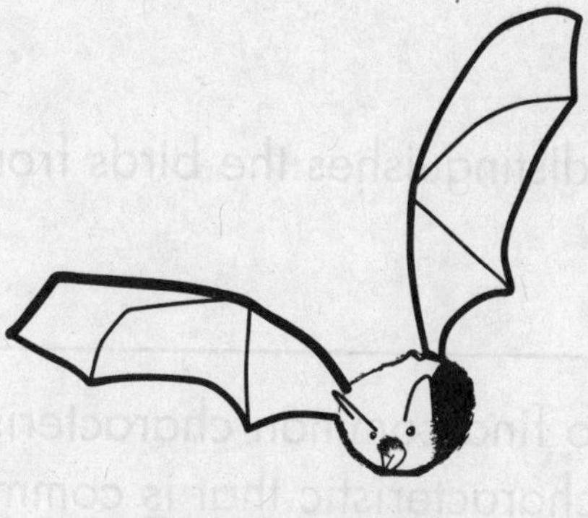

E. Brown Bat

F. Sparrow

What to Do

1. Observe the animal pictures. Compare the characteristics that make these animals alike and different.
2. Use your observations of the animal pictures to fill in the chart on page 10. Write the letter of the animal in the correct column for each question.
3. Think of two other characteristics you can use to classify these animals. Write one question for each characteristic in the chart. Fill in the letters of the animals.

Name ________________________________

Observable Characteristics	Yes	No
1. Is the animal's body covered with fur?		
2. Is the animal's body covered with feathers?		
3. Can the animal fly?		
4. Write your question here:		
5. Write your question here:		

Explain Your Results

1. Which characteristic distinguishes the birds from the other animals?

____

2. Classifying is useful to find common characteristics within a group. Name one characteristic that is common to all birds besides feathers.

____

Name ______________________________

Practice Inferring

Inferring means developing ideas based on observations and experience. Inferences are often used in predictions. They are also used to draw conclusions from data. In this activity, you will use your experience with static electricity to make inferences about the behavior of a balloon and an aluminum can.

Materials

balloon
cloth
empty aluminum can

What to Do

1. Place the can on its side on a level surface.
2. Fill the balloon with air.
3. Based on your observations and past experience, predict what will happen when you hold the balloon near the can. Write your prediction here:

   ____

   ____

4. Hold the balloon about 3 cm from the can. Try to use the balloon to make the can roll back and forth without touching the can with the balloon. Record your observations below.

   ____

5. Rub the balloon on the cloth to build up a static charge. Now try to make the can roll. Record your observations.

   ____

6. Touch the can with the charged balloon, then try to make the can roll. Record your observations.

   ____

   ____

Name ______________________________

Explain Your Results

1. Describe two situations in which you have observed static electricity.

2. Inferences based on past experience are often used to make predictions about the results of an experiment. What inferences about static electricity did you use to predict what would happen when you held the uncharged balloon near the can?

3. Based on your observations and prior experience, make an inference about what happened when you held the balloon near the can after it had been rubbed on the cloth.

Name ______________________________

Practice Predicting

Predicting means using prior knowledge to form an idea of an expected result. In this activity you will predict how far a model car will travel on a ramp.

Materials

cardboard
objects to raise the ramp (such as books)
model car
meterstick
masking tape

What to Do

1. Use two books and the cardboard to make a ramp, as in the illustration at right.

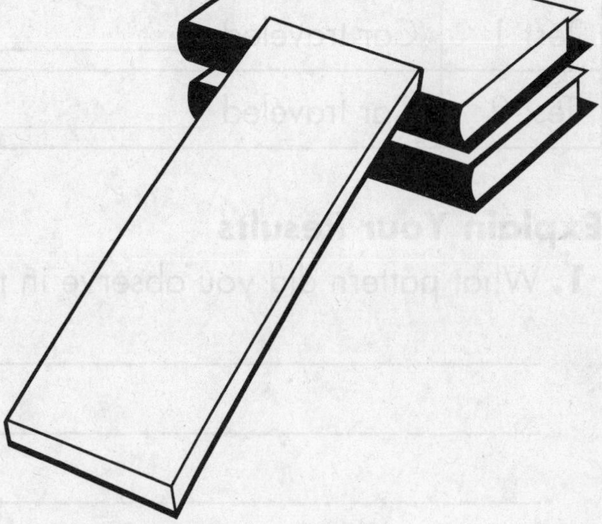

2. Place the model car at the top of the ramp. Gently let go of the car so that it rolls down the ramp and across the floor.
3. Use a piece of masking tape to mark where the car stops. Measure how far the car traveled from the ramp. Record the distance in the chart on page 14 next to Test 1.
4. Repeat steps 2–3. Record your observations in the chart next to Test 2.
5. Now add 1 book to make the ramp higher. Repeat steps 2–4. Record your observations in the chart.
6. Add another book to make the ramp higher. Based on your observations, predict how far you think the car will travel.

   My prediction: The car will travel __________ cm.
7. Repeat steps 2–4.

Name ______________________________

Distance Car Traveled

Trial 1: Ramp set on 2 books.	
Test 1	Car traveled ________
Test 2	Car traveled ________
Trial 2: Ramp set on 3 books.	
Test 1	Car traveled ________
Test 2	Car traveled ________
Trial 3: Ramp set on 4 books.	
Test 1	Car traveled ________
Test 2	Car traveled ________

Explain Your Results

1. What pattern did you observe in the activity?

____

____

____

2. How accurate was your prediction of how far the car would travel in trial 3?

____

3. Why wasn't your prediction completely accurate? List one variable besides the height of the ramp that affected the distance the car traveled in trial 3.

____

____

____

Name ____________________________________

Practice Making and Using Models

Models represent ideas, objects, or events. You will make a model of a food chain and observe a model of a food web. These models show how energy flows among plants and animals.

Materials

paper

glue

pictures of animals

Sun

Owl

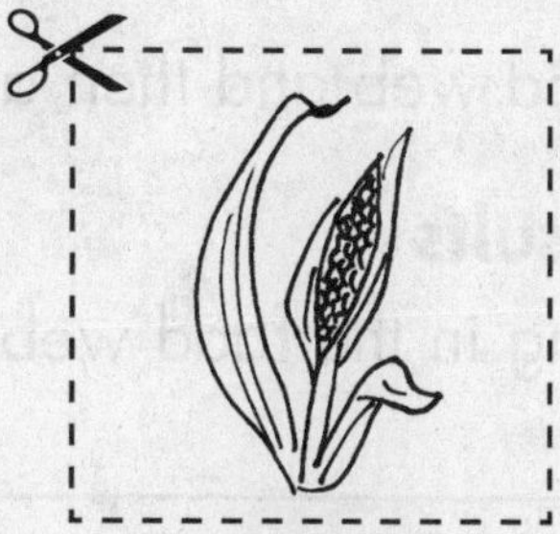

Wheat

Mouse

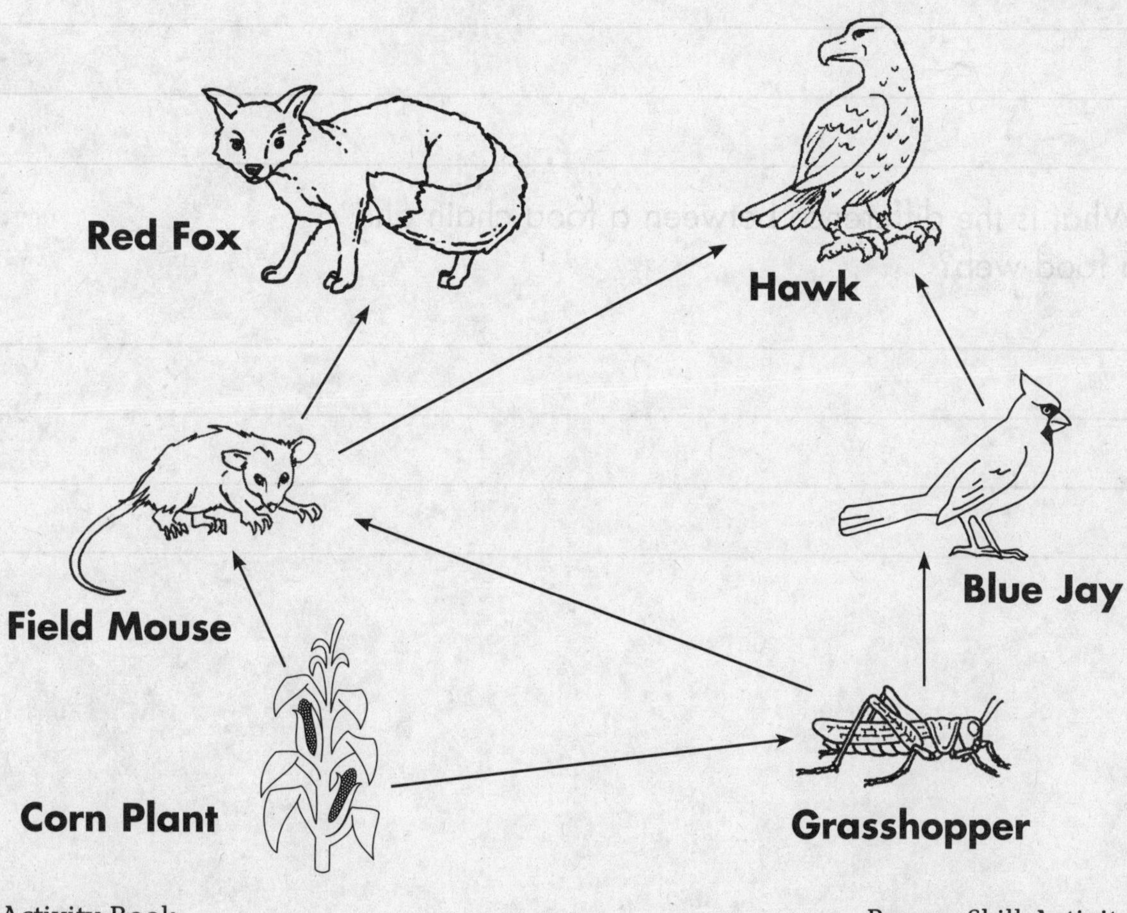

Name ______________________

What to Do

1. Cut out the pictures. Arrange the Sun, owl, wheat plant, and mouse in the correct order to make a food chain. Glue the pictures to your paper and connect them with arrows.
   Explain how the living things in your model food chain are connected.

   ____

   ____

2. Examine the food web and then answer the questions.

Explain Your Results

1. What living thing in the food web makes its own food?

____

2. What living thing is more important to this food web, the corn plant or the red fox? Why?

____

____

____

3. What is the difference between a food chain and a food web?

____

____

____

____

Name ______________________________

Practice Interpreting Data

Interpreting data means explaining what you observed and recorded during an an investigation or experiment. In this activity, you will look for patterns in the data you gather about indoor and outdoor temperatures.

Materials

2 thermometers
2 different colored markers

What to Do

1. Place 1 thermometer outdoors and 1 thermometer indoors. Choose a location indoors for 1 thermometer. Write your location here. Indoor location: __________
   Choose a location outdoors for 1 thermometer. Write your location here. Outdoor location: __________
2. Choose a morning time and an afternoon time to check your thermometers. Record them in the chart.
3. Check your thermometers every morning and afternoon. Record your data in the charts.

Outdoor Temperature	Morning: _____ A.M.	Afternoon: _____ P.M.
Day 1		
Day 2		
Day 3		

Indoor Temperature	Morning: _____ A.M.	Afternoon: _____ P.M.
Day 1		
Day 2		
Day 3		

Name ______________________________

4 Show your data in the line graph. Use different colored markers for the indoor temperature and outdoor temperature.

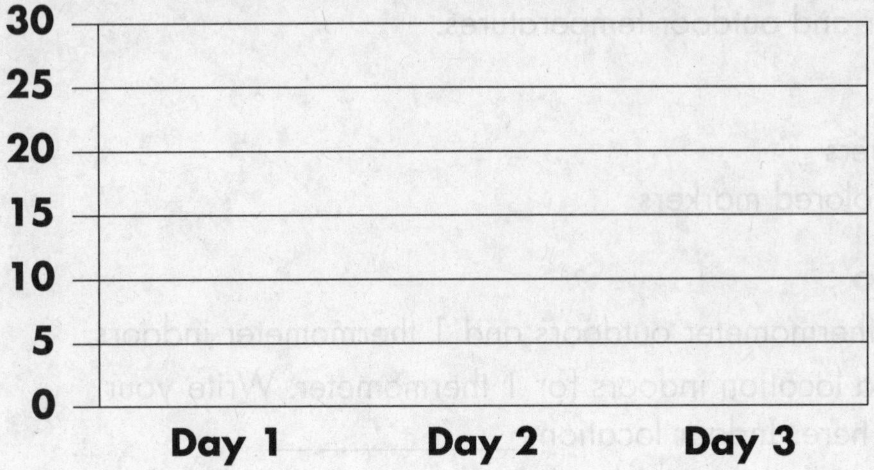

Explain Your Results

1. What day had the lowest indoor temperature? What was the outdoor temperature at that same time? What was the difference between the two temperatures?

____

____

____

2. Were temperatures usually cooler in the morning or in the afternoon? Why?

____

____

3. Observe your line graph. List at least two patterns you find in your data.

____

____

____

____

Name ______________________________

Practice Forming Questions and Hypotheses

Forming hypotheses means phrasing a scientific **question** as a statement that can be tested by an experiment. In this experiment, you will form and test a hypothesis about whether using a ramp will make it easier to lift a weight.

Materials

book	meterstick	cardboard	stapler
ramp	rubber band	string	

What to do

1. If you use a ramp to move an object, will it take less effort than lifting the object vertically? Write your hypothesis below. Make sure your hypothesis can be tested in an experiment.

   ____

   ____

2. Build a ramp 30 cm (12 in.) high.
3. Turn the cardboard lengthwise. Start at the top and use the meterstick to mark 2 cm, 4 cm, 6 cm, 8 cm, and so on up to 24 cm.
4. Staple the rubber band to the top of the cardboard. Measure the length of the rubber band without stretching it. Record your data in the chart on page 20.
5. Place the book at the bottom of the ramp.
6. Use a string to attach the book to the rubber band.
7. Hold the top of the rubber band and pull the book to the top of the ramp. Observe the length of the stretched rubber band as you pull the book. The stretch is a measure of the force needed to move the book. Record your data in the chart.

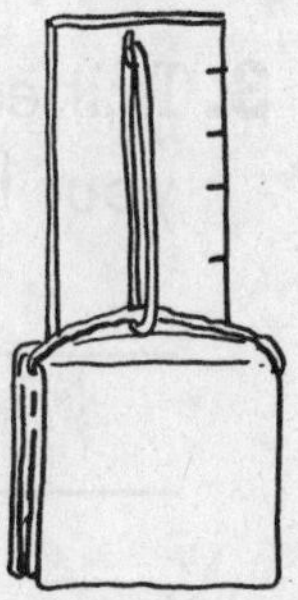

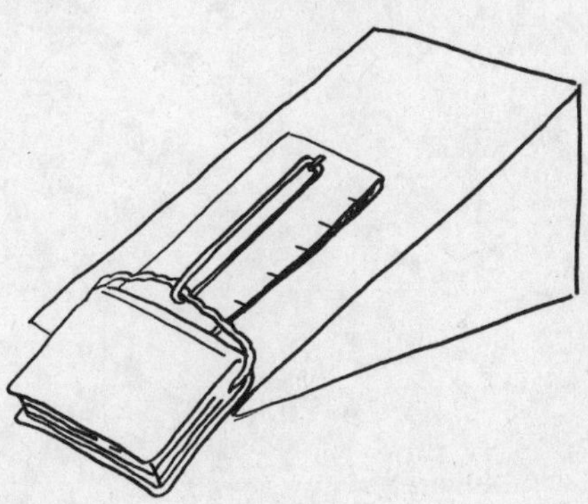

Name ______________________________

8 Lay the book flat on the table.

9 Hold the top of the rubber band and lift the book vertically to a height of 30 cm. Observe the length of the rubber band. Record your data in the chart.

Length of rubber band at rest	
Length of rubber band pulling book up the ramp	
Length of rubber band lifting book vertically	

Explain Your Results

1. Which method of moving the book took more effort?

____

2. Was your hypothesis correct? Why or why not?

____

____

3. Is it easier to pull a book on a metal ramp, or on a wood ramp? State your hypothesis below. Explain.

____

____

____

Name ______________________

Practice Identifying and Controlling Variables

Identifying and controlling variables means changing one factor (independent variable) in an experiment while other variables (controlled) stay the same. In this activity, you will manipulate light to find out if seeds need light to grow.

Materials

2 paper towels
2 lids from wide-mouth jars
10 pinto beans
water, in a pouring container

What to Do

1. You will conduct an experiment to find out if seeds need light to grow. What is the independent variable in this experiment?

____

2. Fold the paper towels to fit into the lid. Place 5 beans on each paper towel.

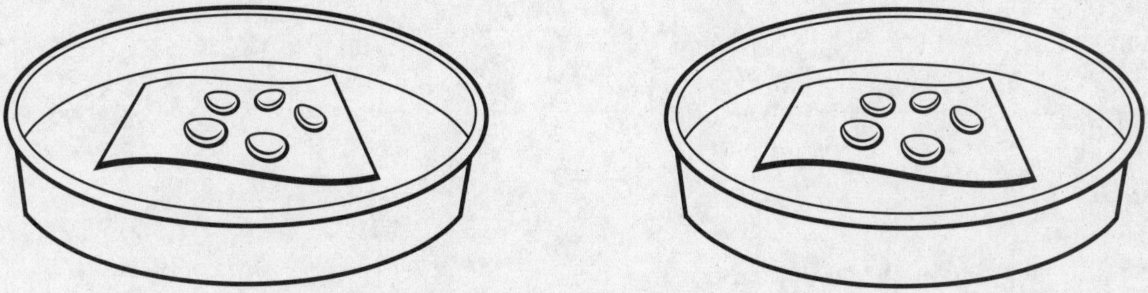

3. Pour water on the towels until they are moist.
4. Place one lid where there is light. Place the other lid in a dark place. Wait 4 days before recording your observations in the chart below.

Location of Seeds	Number of Seeds Sprouted After 4 Days
Light	
No light	

Name ______________________________

Explain Your Results

1. Do pinto beans need light to grow? How do you know?

____

____

____

2. Are your results true of all seeds? Explain.

____

____

____

3. In the experiment, the independent variable was the availability of light. Which variable was affected by light?

____

Practice Making Operational Definitions

Making an operational definition means stating specific information about an object based on your observations and experiences with it. In this activity, you will state information about paper cups by measuring how much weight 6 cups can hold before they collapse.

Materials

6 paper cups, 4 oz size
several books of about the same size
tray
scale

What to Do

1. Place the cups bottom up on a flat surface. Line them up in 2 rows of 3 cups.
2. Place the tray on top of the cups.
3. Predict how many books you think the cups will support.
   ________ books

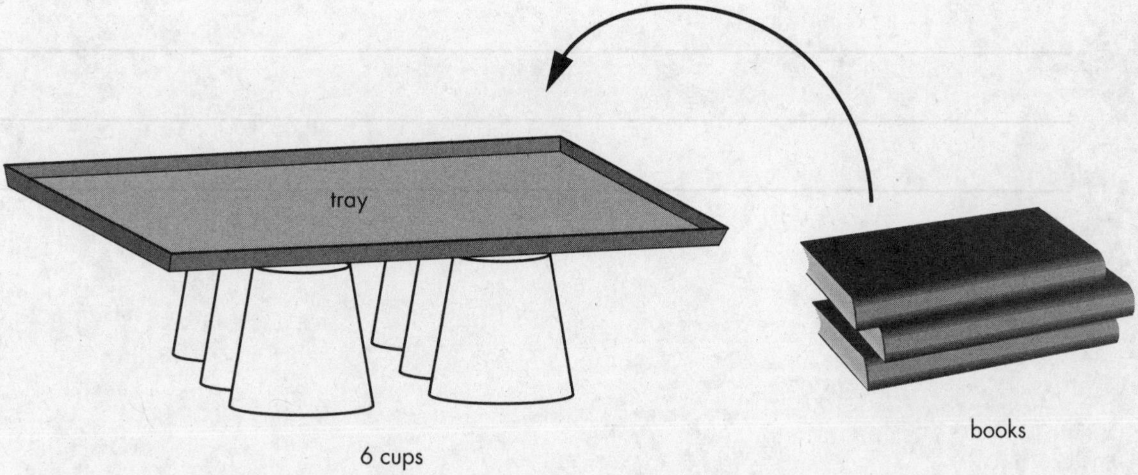

4. Carefully add books to the center of the tray until the cups collapse.
5. Write the number of books supported by the cups here:
   ________ books
6. Use the scale to weigh the books. Write the total weight supported by the cups here:
   ________ kg

Name ____________________

Explain Your Results

1. How many books did the 6 cups support before collapsing? Did the cups hold more or fewer books than you predicted?

____

____

2. Operational definitions describe specific information about an object. Which description of the cups' strength is more specific: the number of books the cups can hold or the weight the cups can hold? Explain your answer.

____

____

3. In this activity, you tested the strength of paper cups by determining how much weight the cups could hold. What is another way to test the strength of paper cups?

____

____

____

Practice Investigating and Experimenting

Experiment means creating a systematic procedure to answer a scientific question and test a hypothesis to form a conclusion. In this activity, you will conduct an experiment to **investigate** how colored lights interact with each other.

Materials

red, green, and blue colored pencils or crayons
white drawing paper
3 flashlights
3 sheets of plastic wrap, 15 cm × 15 cm
- 1 red
- 1 green
- 1 blue

3 rubber bands
white background (wall or large sheet of paper)

What to Do

1. Use the drawing paper and colored pencils or crayons to show what happens when you mix the colors red, green, and blue. Describe your results below.

   ____

   Why did this happen? Explain your results.

   ____

   ____

2. What happens when red light, green light, and blue light are mixed together? Write your hypothesis based on the first question. Make sure your hypothesis can be tested in an experiment.

   ____

   ____

3. Cover the head of each flashlight with a different colored piece of plastic wrap. Use rubber bands to hold the plastic wrap in place.

4 Turn on each flashlight and shine the light on the white background. Observe what color light each flashlight produces. Record your observations here:

Color of plastic wrap on flashlight	Color of light produced by flashlight
Red	
Green	
Blue	

5 Turn off the flashlights and place them on a table facing the white background. Keep the flashlight in the center facing straight ahead.

6 Turn the flashlights on either side slightly toward the one in the center, as in the diagram.

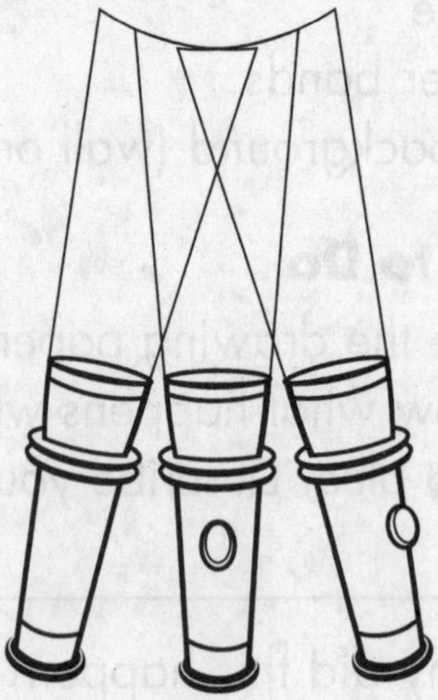

7 Turn the flashlights on. Move the outer flashlights so that the 3 circles of light overlap each other.

8 Draw and color what you observe.

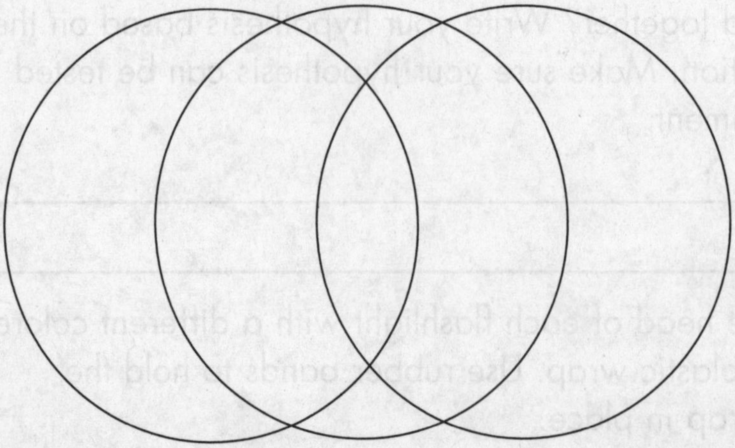

Name ____________________

Explain Your Results

1. Hypotheses are based on inferences about prior knowledge. What prior observations about color did you use to write your hypothesis? Was your hypothesis correct?

2. In step 4, you shone each flashlight on a white background and recorded the color of light that was produced. Why was this step necessary?

3. Do you think your results would be the same if you used red, orange, and yellow plastic wrap? Why or why not?

Name ______________________________

Use with Chapter 1, p. 4

Explore: What are living things made of?

Explain Your Results

1. Draw what you **observed.**

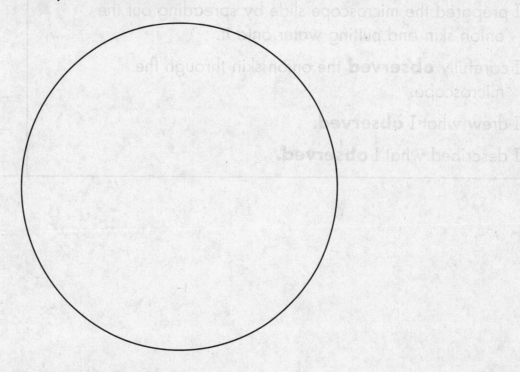

2. Describe what you observed.

____

____

____

Name ________________________________

Use with Chapter 1, p. 4

Self-Assessment Checklist	
I followed instructions to separate the layers of an onion.	_____
I prepared the microscope slide by spreading out the onion skin and putting water onto it.	_____
I carefully **observed** the onion skin through the microscope.	_____
I drew what I **observed.**	_____
I described what I **observed.**	_____

Notes for Home: Your child **observed** the skin of an onion under a microscope.
Home Activity: With your child, discuss why each cell has its own nucleus.

Name ______________________

Investigate: How can you use a chart to classify a set of objects?

❶–❸ Follow the **classification** chart on page 35 of your text to identify the leaves.

Identification Chart	
Leaf	**Name**
Leaf A	
Leaf B	
Leaf C	
Leaf D	
Leaf E	
Leaf F	

Explain Your Results

1. List the features you used to **classify** the leaves.

____

2. What other features could you use to classify leaves?

____

Go Further

How could you use a chart to classify a group of animals? Make a plan to answer this or other questions you may have.

____

____

____

Name ______________________________

Guided Inquiry

Use with Chapter 1, pp. 34–35.

Self-Assessment Checklist	
I **observed** the leaf pictures.	______
I followed the **classification** chart to identify the leaves.	______
I wrote the name of each leaf in the identification chart.	______
I listed the features I used to **classify** my leaves.	______
I identified other features I could use to **classify** leaves.	______

Notes for Home: Your child did an activity to identify tree leaves using a classification chart.
Home Activity: With your child, discuss why leaves have different shapes.

Lab zone **Activity**

What is the structure of a feather?

Materials

What to Do

1. **Observe** the long contour feather. Gently separate the pieces that branch off the shaft, but do not pull them off. Observe the feather with the hand lens. Draw what you see.

2. Use the hand lens to examine how each of the barbs on the feather fit together. Draw what you see.

3. Ruffle the edge of the feather. Observe what happens to the barbs.

4. Now smooth the feather and record what happens to the barbs.

5. Cut the contour feather through the thicker part of its shaft. Use the hand lens to observe the cut ends of the feather. Draw what the shaft looks like inside.

6. Observe the fluffy down feather with the hand lens. Draw what you see.

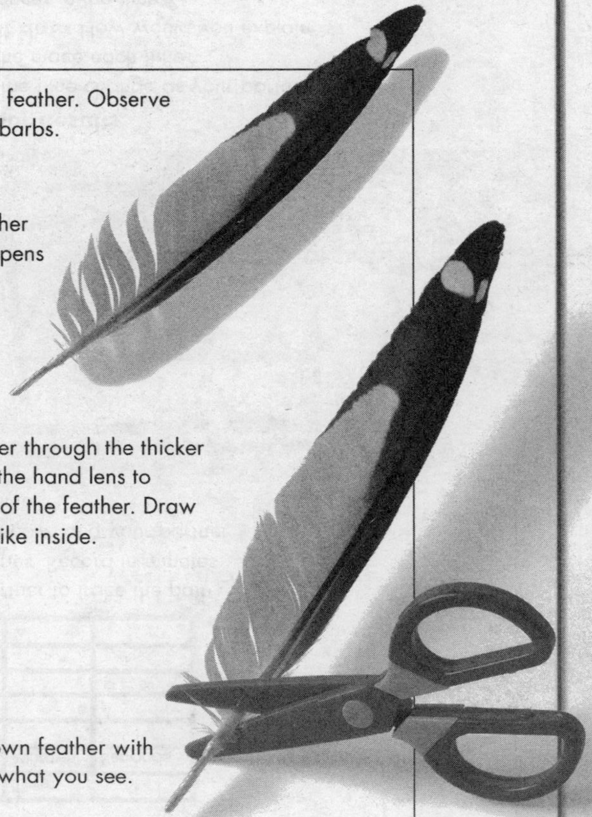

Process Skills

When you **observe** something, you find out how it looks, smells, sounds, feels, or tastes.

Explain Your Results

1. **Observe** How are the feathers alike? How are they different?
2. **Infer** How do you think the hollow shaft helps a bird fly?

Use with Chapter 1

1

Lab zone **Activity**

How can you learn by trial and error?

Materials

What to Do

1. With a pencil, draw a finger maze on a large sheet of paper. Your maze should have a starting place, a finish, one path that leads to the finish, and several paths with dead ends. Make the maze as difficult as you can. Do not show the maze to your partner.

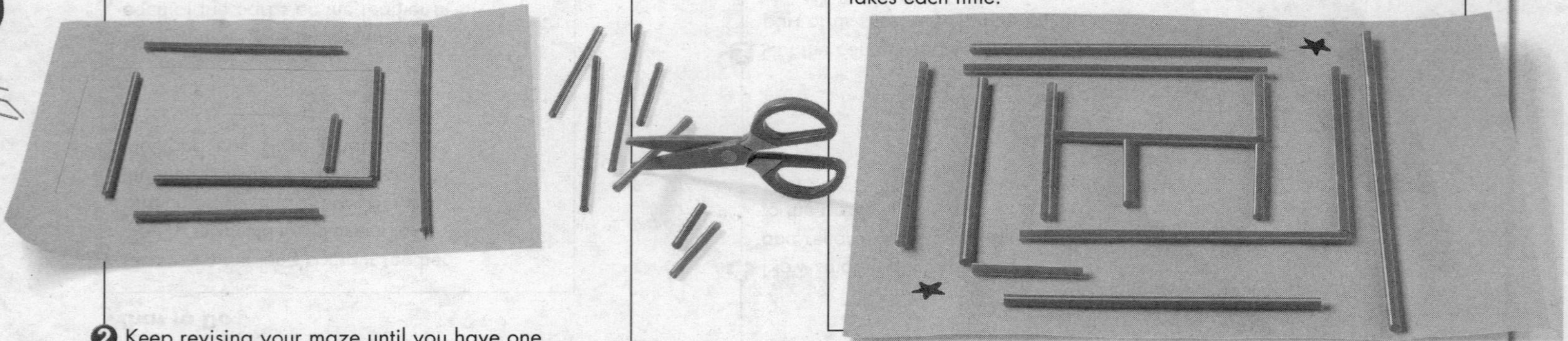

2. Keep revising your maze until you have one that you think will be difficult to follow. Cut straws to fit on the maze lines. Glue on the straws and let the glue dry. Label the Start and Finish.

3. Give the maze to your partner. **Collect data.** Time how long your partner takes to find and move a finger along the correct path from Start to Finish. Record the time in minutes and seconds.

Trial	Time	
	Minutes	Seconds
1		
2		
3		
4		
5		

4. Ask your partner to trace the path four more times. Record in minutes and seconds how long your partner takes each time.

Explain Your Results

1. How did the time change as your partner traveled the maze each time?
2. **Interpret data** How would you explain the differences in the times?

Process Skills

You can **collect and interpret data** to answer questions.

Use with Chapter 1

2

Name ______________________

What is the structure of a feather?

❶ **Observe** the long contour feather. Gently separate the pieces that branch off the shaft, but do not pull them off. Observe the feather with the hand lens. Draw what you see.

❷ Use the hand lens to examine how each of the barbs on the feather fit together. Draw what you see.

❸–❹ Ruffle the edges of the feather. Now smooth the feather and record what happens to the barbs.

____

____

❺ Cut the contour feather in half through the thicker part of its shaft. Use the hand lens to observe the cut ends of the feather. Draw what the shaft looks like inside.

Name ____________________

❻ Observe the fluffy down feather with the hand lens. Draw what you see.

Explain Your Results

1. Observe: How are the feathers alike? How are they different?

____

____

2. Infer: How do you think the hollow shaft helps a bird fly?

____

____

Self-Assessment Checklist	
I **observed** the long contour feather and its barbs when the feather was ruffled and smooth.	____
I cut the contour feather in half and **observed** the ends with a hand lens.	____
I **observed** the fluffy down feather with the hand lens.	____
I **observed** how the feathers are alike and how they are different.	____
I made an **inference** about how the hollow shaft helps a bird fly.	____

Notes for Home: Your child did an activity to examine the structure of a feather.
Home Activity: With your child, discuss what the different functions of feathers are.

Name ______________________

How can you learn by trial and error?

❸–❹ Give the maze to your partner. **Collect data.** Time how long your partner takes to find and move a finger along the correct path from Start to Finish. Record the time in minutes and seconds in the chart. Ask your partner to trace the path four more times. Record in minutes and seconds how long your partner takes each time.

Trial	Time	
	Minutes	Seconds
1		
2		
3		
4		
5		

Explain Your Results

1. How did the time change as your partner traveled the maze each time?

____

2. **Interpret Data:** How would you explain the differences in the times?

____

____

Name ______________________

Self-Assessment Checklist	
I followed instructions to create a finger maze on a large sheet of paper.	____
I **collected data** about how long it took my partner to complete the maze.	____
I recorded my partner's time for each of the 4 additional trials.	____
I described how the time changed as my partner moved through the maze each time.	____
I **interpreted my data** to explain the differences in times.	____

Notes for Home: Your child did an activity to explore how someone can learn through trial and error.
Home Activity: With your child, think of an example of something else your child learned by trial and error.

Name ______________________

Use with Chapter 2, p. 44

Explore: How can you show that a plant needs light?

3 Record your **observations** of the covered and uncovered leaves.

Covered leaves: ______________________

____

Uncovered leaves: ______________________

____

Explain Your Results

Compare your **observations** of the leaves and draw a conclusion. What do you think might have caused the leaves to look different?

____

____

____

____

Self-Assessment Checklist	
I followed instructions to cover a leaf on my plant.	______
I placed the plant in a sunny place and watered it every other day for a week.	______
I recorded my **observations** of the covered and uncovered leaves.	______
I compared my **observations** of the covered and uncovered leaves.	______
I drew a conclusion about what caused the leaves to look different.	______

Notes for Home: Your child did an activity to show that a plant needs light.
Home Activity: With your child, discuss how you might show that a plant needs water to grow.

Name ______________________________

Lab zone **Guided Inquiry**

Use with Chapter 2, pp. 66–67

Investigate: How can you grow a potato plant without a seed?

3–4 Observe the potato daily for 2 weeks. Draw or describe what you observe.

Draw Your Observations		
At the Start	**After 7 Days**	**After 14 Days**

Explain Your Results

1. Based on what you have **observed, predict** what might happen to a potato left for 2 weeks in damp soil. Explain the evidence for your prediction.

____

____

____

____

____

____

2. Infer: Why might a potato farmer save part of a crop?

____

3. How are observations, inferences, and predictions different from one another?

____

____

____

____

Go Further

How could you grow other plants, such as carrots or houseplants, without seeds? Make a plan to investigate this or other questions you may have.

____

____

Self-Assessment Checklist	
I followed instructions to put toothpicks in a potato, placed the potato in a cup of water, and added water to the cup as needed.	____
I **observed** the potato for 2 weeks and drew or described what I **observed.**	____
I **predicted** what might happen to a potato left in damp soil and supported my prediction.	____
I made an **inference** about why a potato farmer might save part of a crop.	____
I described how observations, inferences, and predictions are different from each other.	____

Notes for Home: Your child did an activity to grow a potato plant without a seed.
Home Activity: With your child, discuss how other plants can be grown without seeds.

Lab zone **Activity**

How can you move a seed?

Materials

Process Skills

When you make and **use models,** you use objects and materials to represent something else.

What to Do

1. Place 5 lima beans at one end of the pan.
2. Think about how you could move the seeds to the other end of the pan without touching them. You can use any of the materials provided. Make a list of your ideas.
3. Try each method on your list. Record whether you were able to move the seeds with each try.
4. Remove the lima beans from the tray. Put 5 walnuts in the pan.
5. Repeat steps 2 and 3 with the walnuts.

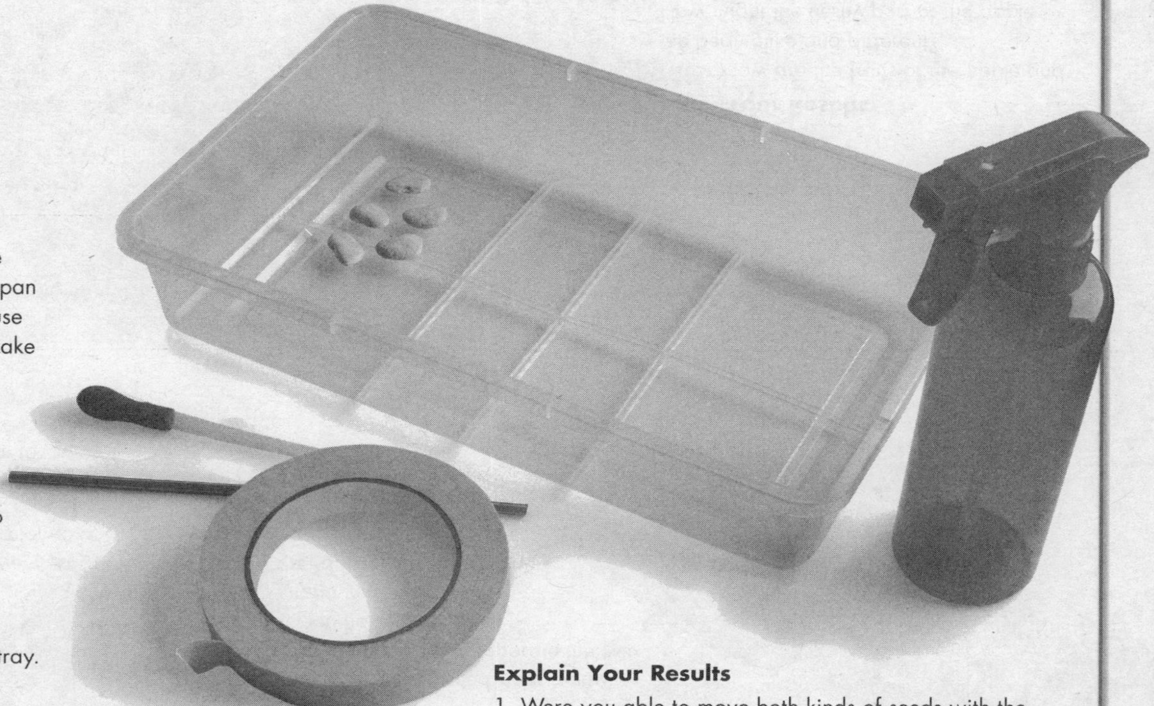

Explain Your Results

1. Were you able to move both kinds of seeds with the same methods? Why do you think this is so?
2. **Make Models** What natural processes to move seeds were modeled with each method you chose?
3. **Predict** Look at pictures of seeds. Which methods do you think could be used to move each seed?

Use with Chapter 2

3

Name ______________________________

Lab zone Activity

What are the parts of a fruit?

Materials

apple

paper plate

lima bean pod

hand lens

plastic knife

Process Skills

When you **make an operational definition,** you state specific information about an object or event based on your experiences with it.

What to Do

1. **Observe** the apple. Find the small sunken area on its bottom. This is where the petals of the flower were attached before the fruit developed.
2. Place the apple on a paper plate. Cut the apple in half from the stem to the bottom. Draw what you see.
3. Remove an apple seed and place it under the flat side of the knife. Push down on the knife on top of the seed. This will cause the seed to separate into two halves. With the hand lens, observe the seed. Draw what you see.

Be careful! Do not eat any food from this activity.

4. Observe the bean pod. Carefully remove one side of the bean pod. Make a drawing of what you see.
5. Remove a bean seed. Tear away the seed coat, and separate the two bean halves. With the hand lens, observe the seed. Look for the embryo.

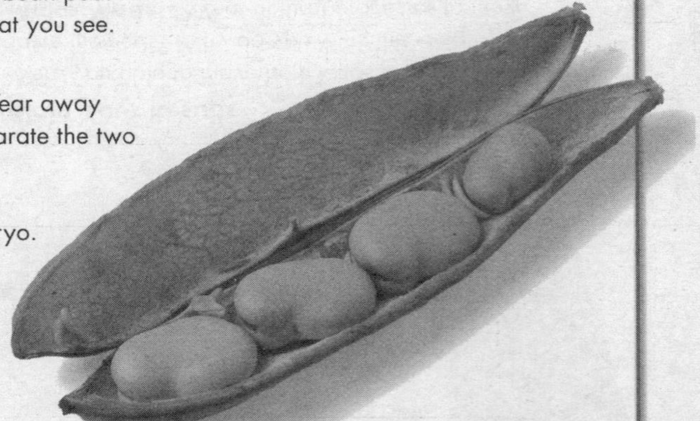

Explain Your Results

1. **Infer** How are the fruits of the apple and the bean alike and different?
2. How might the fleshy part of the apple help its seeds become scattered?
3. **Making Operational Definitions** Use what you observed in this activity to write a definition of a fruit.

Use with Chapter 2

4

Name ______________________

How can you move a seed?

❷–❸ Think about how you could move the seeds to the other end of the pan without touching them. You can use any of the materials provided. Make a list of your ideas in the chart. Try each method on your list. Record whether you were able to move the seeds with each try.

Ideas to move the seeds	Results (moved/did not move)	
	Lima beans	Walnuts

❺ Repeat steps 2 and 3 with the walnuts.

Explain Your Results

1. Were you able to move both kinds of seeds with the same methods? Why do you think this is so?

____

____

____

2. **Make Models:** What natural processes to move seeds were modeled with each method you chose?

____

____

____

Name ______________________________

Use with page 3

3. Predict: Look at pictures of seeds. Which methods do you think could be used to move each seed?

____

____

Self-Assessment Checklist	
I made a list of how I could move the lima beans, tested each method, and recorded my results.	____
I repeated my methods with the walnuts and recorded my results.	____
I explained why I was not able to move both kinds of seeds with the same methods.	____
I described what natural processes to move seeds were **modeled** with each method I chose.	____
I **predicted** which methods could be used to move seeds I saw in pictures.	____

Notes for Home: Your child did an activity to come up with different ways to move seeds.
Home Activity: With your child, find some seeds on plants in your neighborhood and discuss how they move.

Name ______________________

Use with page 4

What are the parts of a fruit?

2. Cut the apple in half from the stem to the bottom. Draw what you see.

3. Remove an apple seed and place it under the flat side of the knife. Push down on the knife on top of the seed. This will cause the seed to separate into two halves. With the hand lens, observe the seed. Draw what you see.

4. Observe the bean pod. Carefully remove one side of the bean pod. Make a drawing of what you see.

Name ______________________________

Activity Flip Chart

Use with page 4

Explain Your Results

1. Infer: How are the fruits of the apple and the bean alike and different?

____

____

2. How might the fleshy part of the apple help its seeds become scattered?

____

____

3. Making Operational Definitions: Use what you observed in the fruits in this activity to write a definition of a fruit.

____

Self-Assessment Checklist	
I drew the inside of the apple and observed the seed.	____
I drew the inside of the bean pod and observed the seed.	____
I made an **inference** about how the fruits of the apple and the bean are alike and different.	____
I described how the fleshy part of the apple might help its seeds become scattered.	____
I **made an operational definition** of a fruit.	____

Notes for Home: Your child did an activity to examine the parts of a fruit.
Home Activity: With your child, list 3 characteristics most vegetables have in common.

Name ____________________

Use with Chapter 3, p. 76

Explore: How can you make a model of an earthworm habitat?

3–4 **Observe** sand, dirt, and earthworms daily for 4 days.

Explain Your Results

1. What changes did you **observe?**

2. How do you think earthworms might get the energy and water they need?

Self-Assessment Checklist	
I added sand and earthworms to my earthworm bottle.	______
I covered the bottle with black paper and foil.	______
I removed the foil and paper, **observed** the sand, dirt, and earthworms, and re-covered the bottle daily for 4 days.	______
I described the changes I **observed.**	______
I **made an inference** about how earthworms get the energy and water they need.	______

Notes for Home: Your child did an activity to **observe** how earthworms meet their needs.
Home Activity: With your child, discuss why more earthworms live in flower gardens than desert sand.

Name ______________________

Lab zone **Guided Inquiry**

Use with Chapter 3, pp. 96–97

Investigate: What do decomposers do?

❹ Look at the bread every day for 10 days. Record what you **observe.**

Day	Observations	
	Damp Bread	**Dry Bread**
Day 1		
Day 2		
Day 3		
Day 4		
Day 5		
Day 6		
Day 7		
Day 8		
Day 9		
Day 10		

Explain Your Results

1. Which slice had more mold? What changes did you **observe?**

____

____

____

____

2. Infer: How does water affect the growth of mold? Where does the mold get the matter and energy it needs?

____

____

____

Go Further

How does mold grow in other conditions, such as cold or dry environments? Make a plan to investigate.

____

Self-Assessment Checklist	
I followed instructions to prepare bread slices and put them in sealed plastic bags.	____
I **observed** the bread slices for 10 days and recorded **data** in the chart.	____
I reported which slice had more mold and described the changes I **observed.**	____
I made an **inference** about how water affects the growth of mold.	____
I made an **inference** about where mold gets the matter and energy it needs.	____

Notes for Home: Your child did an activity to **observe** how mold decomposes bread.
Home Activity: With your child, discuss why freezing foods prevents mold from growing.

Lab zone **Activity**

How are organisms connected in a food chain?

Materials

- 9 index cards
- crayons or markers
- paper punch
- yarn
- metric ruler
- scissors

What to Do

1. Write each of the following plant and animal names on its own index card: grass, garter snake, squirrel, mouse, acorn, corn, hawk, fox, and crow.

2. With the paper punch, make a hole in the top and bottom of each card.

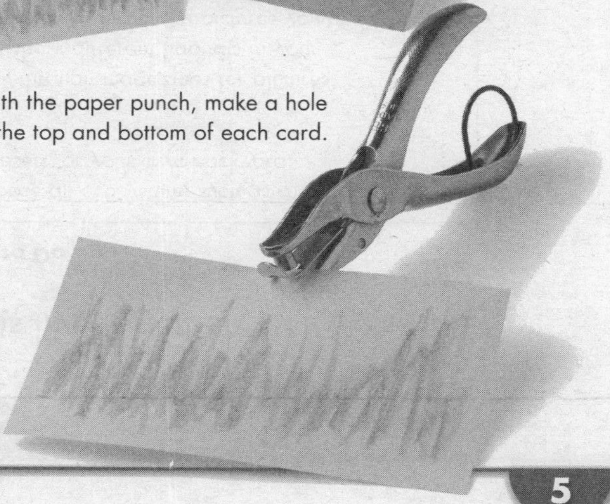

3. Place the three cards with plant names on the desk or table. Below each plant card, place a card with the name of an animal that might eat the plant.

4. Below each of those animal cards, place a card with an animal that might eat it.

5. Cut 6 pieces of yarn, each about 10 cm long. Tie each card to the one above it with a piece of yarn. You have **made models** of three food chains. Record your food chains.

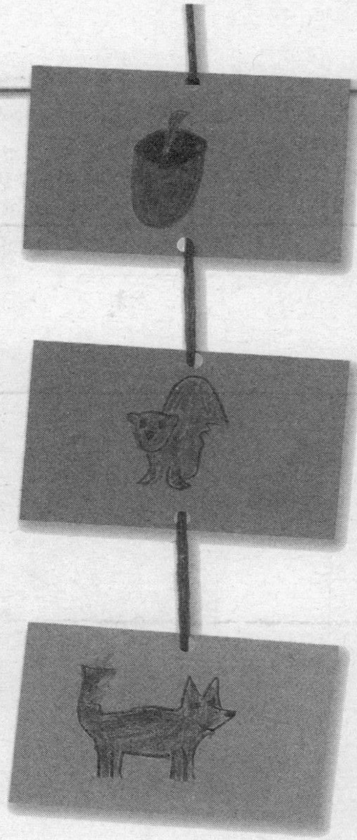

Explain Your Results

1. How are the food chains alike?
2. **Predict** What would happen if you removed the mouse from your food chain?

Process Skills

You **predict** when you form an idea about an expected result.

Lab zone **Activity**

How do organisms live together?

Materials

old magazines
scissors and glue
index card
large sheet of construction paper
colored markers

Process Skills

You can **communicate** your ideas by giving information in a visual and written display.

What to Do

1. Choose an ecosystem, such as a forest, a desert, or your own backyard.
2. Look through magazines for pictures that show different habitats in your ecosystem. Cut out the pictures you find.
3. Cut out other pictures that show individuals, populations, and communities within your ecosystem. Be sure to include some plants.

4. **Communicate** information about your ecosystem. Write a description of it on the index card.
5. Glue the index card and pictures to the sheet of construction paper to make a visual display about your ecosystem. Label the populations and communities.

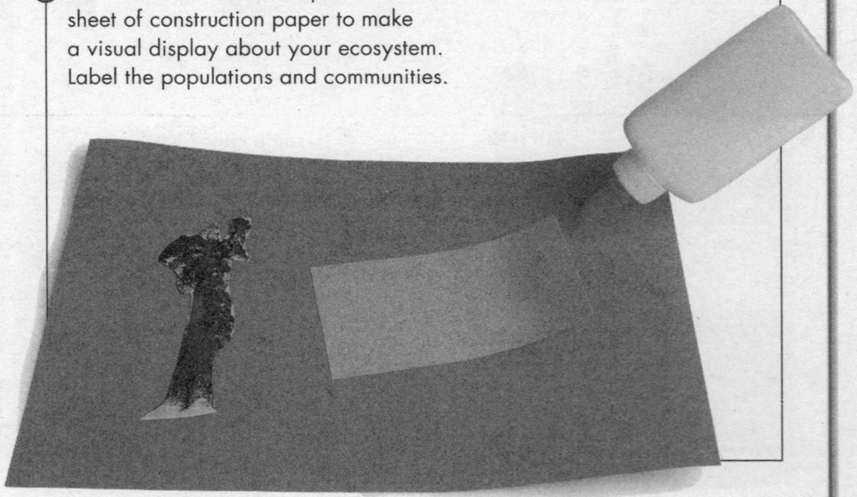

Explain Your Results

1. Choose one organism pictured in your display. Describe at least two adaptations of each organism. Tell how each adaptation helps the organism survive in the ecosystem.
2. **Communicate** Write a few sentences that explain how at least two of the organisms in your ecosystem interact.

Use with Chapter 3

6

Name ________________________

Use with page 5

How are organisms connected in a food chain?

❻ Cut 6 pieces of yarn, each about 10 cm long. Tie each card to the one above it with a piece of yarn. You have **made models** of three food chains. Record your food chains.

Explain Your Results

1. How are the food chains alike?

____

____

2. Predict: What would happen if you removed the mouse from your food chain?

____

____

____

Name ______________________

Use with page 5

Self-Assessment Checklist	
I followed instructions to prepare the cards.	_____
I **made a model** of three food chains.	_____
I recorded my food chains.	_____
I described how the food chains are alike.	_____
I **predicted** what would happen if I removed the mouse from my food chain.	_____

Notes for Home: Your child did an activity to explore how different animals are connected in a food chain.
Home Activity: With your child, think of another food chain that occurs in your local ecosystem.

Use with page 6

How do organisms live together?

Explain Your Results

1. Choose one organism pictured in your display. Describe at least two adaptations of the organism. Tell how each adaptation helps the organism survive in the ecosystem.

____

____

____

____

2. **Communicate:** Write a few sentences that explain how at least two of the organisms in your ecosystem interact.

____

____

____

Self-Assessment Checklist	
I found pictures that showed different habitats and organisms in an ecosystem.	______
I **communicated** information about my ecosystem by writing a description.	______
I made a visual display about my ecosystem and labeled the populations and communities.	______
I described two adaptations of an organism in my display and how each adaptation helps it survive.	______
I **communicated** how at least two of the organisms in my ecosystem interact.	______

Notes for Home: Your child did an activity to make a display showing how organisms in an ecosystem interact.
Home Activity: With your child, name two human adaptations and describe how they are useful.

Name ______________________________

Lab zone **Directed Inquiry**

Use with Chapter 4, p. 108

Explore: What is the effect of crowding on plants?

❹ **Collect data** about the number and appearance of your radish plants.

Day	10 Radish Seeds		80 Radish Seeds	
	Number of Plants	Appearance of Plants	Number of Plants	Appearance of Plants
Day 1				
Day 4				
Day 7				
Day 10				
Day 13				
Day 16				
Day 19				
Day 21				

Name ____________________

Use with Chapter 4, p. 108

Explain Your Results

Based on your **observations,** which cup has healthier plants after 3 weeks? Explain.

____

____

Self-Assessment Checklist	
I followed instructions to set up and plant two pots of seeds.	____
I followed instructions to water the radish plants during the experiment.	____
I **observed** changes in the radish plants.	____
I recorded **data** about the number and appearance of radish plants.	____
I determined which cup had healthier plants after 3 weeks and gave a possible explanation.	____

Notes for Home: Your child did an activity about the effect of overcrowding on radish plants.
Home Activity: With your child, discuss the effects of overcrowding on humans.

Name ____________________

Use with Chapter 4, pp. 130–131

Investigate: How can a change in the environment affect plant growth?

❺ **Collect data.** Every day record how many radish plants are in each cup.

Effect of Salt on Radish Plants			
Day	**Number of Radish Plants**		
	Cup A (tap water)	**Cup B (salty water)**	**Cup C (very salty water)**
Day 1			
Day 2			
Day 3			
Day 4			
Day 5			
Day 6			
Day 7			
Day 8			
Day 9			
Day 10			

Explain Your Results

1. How did salt in the environment change how radish plants grew?

____

2. Infer: How might a buildup of salt in the soil affect a farmer?

____

____

Go Further

Are there plants that can grow in salty soils? Make a plan to investigate this or other questions you may have.

____

____

____

____

Self-Assessment Checklist	
I followed instructions to prepare cups with radish plants and water them every day.	____
I **observed** the growth of the radish plants.	____
I **collected data** by recording in a chart the number of radish plants in each cup.	____
I drew conclusions about the effect of salt in the environment on radish plants.	____
I made an **inference** about how a build up of salt in the soil would affect a farmer's crops.	____

Notes for Home: Your child did an activity about the effect of salt on radish plants.
Home Activity: With your child, discuss other pollutants that affect plant growth.

Lab zone Activity

Can you find fossils in pea gravel?

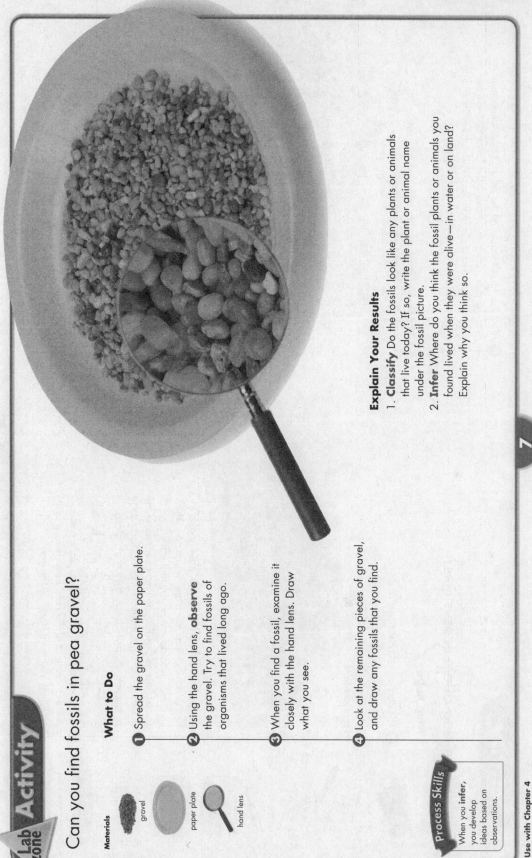

Materials

gravel

paper plate

hand lens

What to Do

1. Spread the gravel on the paper plate.
2. Using the hand lens, **observe** the gravel. Try to find fossils of organisms that lived long ago.
3. When you find a fossil, examine it closely with the hand lens. Draw what you see.
4. Look at the remaining pieces of gravel, and draw any fossils that you find.

Explain Your Results

1. **Classify** Do the fossils look like any plants or animals that live today? If so, write the plant or animal name under the fossil picture.
2. **Infer** Where do you think the fossil plants or animals you found lived when they were alive—in water or on land? Explain why you think so.

Process Skills

When you **infer,** you develop ideas based on observations.

Name ______________________

Activity Flip Chart

Use with Chapter 4

Lab zone **Activity**

How does mining affect ecosystems?

Materials

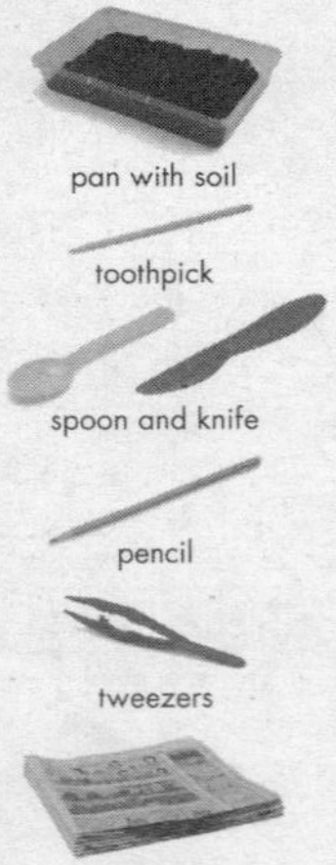

What to Do

1. The pan of soil is a model of a mining site. Sunflower seeds have been buried in the soil. The seeds represent ore.

2. You will **model** mining for ore. Your goal is to find and remove as much ore as you can. The challenge is to do it in a way that affects the soil as little as possible. You may use any of the materials shown in the materials list. Record the procedure you plan to use, then start mining.

3. As you locate and mine the ore, place each piece at one end of the pan. Keep mining until you think you have found all the ore.

4. After you have located all the seeds, break them open over the pan to model removing the "minerals" inside the ore. The seed shells represent wastes from the mining process. Place the minerals beside the pan.

5. **Observe** your mining site after you complete the activity. Record your observations.

Process Skills

A **prediction** can be made from what you learn when **using a model.**

Explain Your Results

1. **Observe** How did finding and removing the seeds affect the soil?
2. **Infer** How do you think mining can affect land and organisms at a mining site?
3. **Predict** How easy do you think it would be to change the mining site back to the way it was before mining?

Use with Chapter 4

8

Name ______________________

Use with page 7

Can you find fossils in pea gravel?

3–4 When you find a fossil, examine it closely with the hand lens. Draw what you see. Look at the remaining pieces of gravel, and draw any fossils that you find.

Explain Your Results

1. **Classify:** Do the fossils look like any plants or animals that live today? If so, write the name of the present day plant or animal under the fossil picture.

2. Infer: Where do you think the fossil plants or animals you found lived when they were alive—in water or on land? Explain why you think so.

____

____

____

Self-Assessment Checklist	
I followed instructions to spread the gravel on the paper plate.	____
I **observed** the gravel with the hand lens and tried to find fossils.	____
I examined the fossils I found with the hand lens and drew what I saw.	____
I **classified** the fossils by naming the present day plant or animal they look like.	____
I made an **inference** about where the fossil plants or animals lived when they were alive.	____

Notes for Home: Your child did an activity to find and **observe** fossils in pea gravel.
Home Activity: With your child, find out what kinds of organisms lived in your area millions of years ago.

How does mining affect ecosystems?

❷ You will **model** mining for ore. Your goal is to find and remove as much ore as you can. The challenge is to do it in a way that affects the soil as little as possible. You may use any of the materials shown in the materials list. Record the procedure you plan to use.

____

____

❺ **Observe** your mining site after you complete the activity. Record your observations.

____

Explain Your Results

1. Observe: How did finding and removing the seeds affect the soil?

____

2. Infer: How do you think mining can affect land and organisms at a mining site?

____

____

____

3. Predict: How easy do you think it would be to change the mining site back to the way it was before mining?

____

____

____

____

Name ______________________________

Activity Flip Chart

Use with page 8

Self-Assessment Checklist	
I came up with a procedure to remove sunflower seeds from the **model** mine.	____
I followed instructions to place the seeds at one end of the pan and to break them open.	____
I **observed** how finding and removing the seeds affected the soil.	____
I made an **inference** about how mining can affect the land and organisms at a mining site.	____
I **predicted** how easy it would be to change the mining site back to the way it was.	____

Notes for Home: Your child did an activity to **use a model** that shows how mining affects ecosystems.
Home Activity: With your child, find pictures of a site that has been mined.

Name ______________________

Lab zone **Directed Inquiry**

Use with Chapter 5, p. 140

Explore: How does shape affect bone strength?

Explain Your Results

1. Which tube held more books?

____

2. Infer: Which is a stronger shape for bones?

____

____

Self-Assessment Checklist	
I followed instructions to form 1 round tube and 1 square tube from construction paper.	____
I followed instructions to stand the tubes on the table and place a book on top of each.	____
I carefully added books to each tube, 1 at a time, until 1 tube collapsed.	____
I **observed** which tube held more books.	____
I made an **inference** about which is a stronger shape for bones.	____

Notes for Home: Your child did an activity to find out how shape affects bone strength.
Home Activity: With your child, discuss why the spine is made up of separate continuous bones instead of one long cylinder.

Name ______________________________

Lab zone **Guided Inquiry**

Use with Chapter 5, pp. 162–163

Investigate: How can some diseases be spread?

❹ Look at the sheets through a hand lens. Draw what you **observe.**

How Pathogens Can Pass from Hand to Hand

Sheet	Drawing of Observations
Sheet A	
Sheet B	
Sheet C	
Sheet D	

Name ____________________

Lab zone **Guided Inquiry**

Use with Chapter 5, pp. 162–163

Explain Your Results

1. What can you **infer** from your **model** about how pathogens pass from person to person?

____

____

____

2. Why do you think doctors wash their hands in between seeing different patients?

____

____

____

Go Further

How could washing your hands affect the spread of some diseases? Make a plan using your model to answer this or other questions you may have.

____

____

Self-Assessment Checklist	
I followed instructions to **make a model** of how some diseases spread.	_____
I **observed** the sheets through a hand lens.	_____
I drew what I **observed** in the chart.	_____
I made an **inference** about how pathogens pass from person to person.	_____
I made an **inference** about why doctors wash their hands in between seeing different patients.	_____

Notes for Home: Your child did an activity to show how diseases can pass from one individual to another.
Home Activity: With your child, discuss how germs spread through the air.

Name ____________________

Lab zone Activity

How can your fingers move?

What to Do

1. Place your hand on a table so that it rests on your fingertips. Bend the center finger under.

2. Try to lift your other fingers, one by one. Which fingers could you move without moving any other fingers? Record your **observations.**

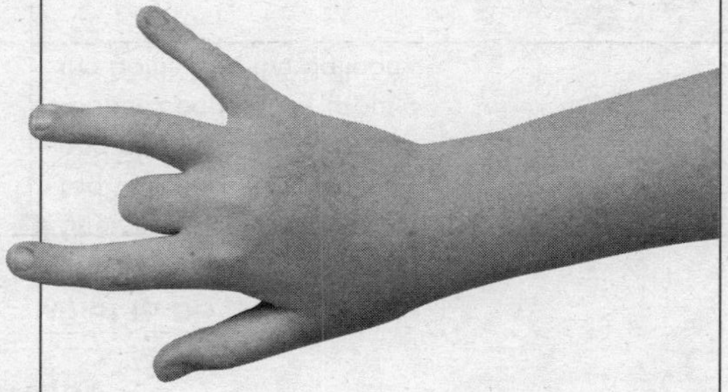

Process Skills

You can **observe** how your fingers move.

3. Place your hand palm down on the table. Try to lift your fingers one by one. Which fingers could you move without moving any other finger?

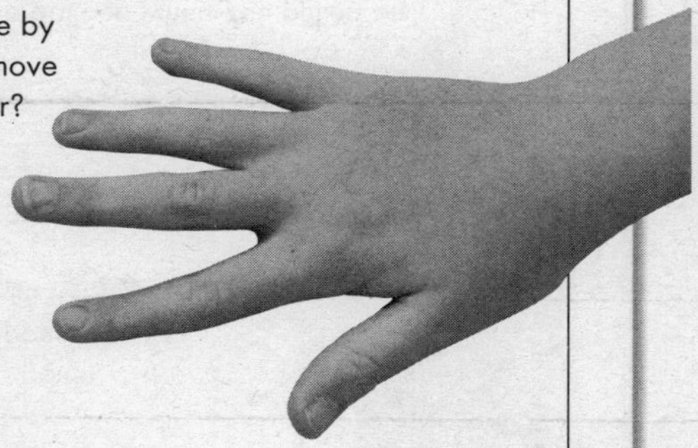

4. Turn your hand over so that it rests on the table palm up. Try to lift your fingers one by one. Which fingers could you move without moving any other finger?

Explain Your Results

1. Describe your **observations.**
2. Did your observations surprise you? Explain.

Use with Chapter 5

9

Name ______________________________

Lab zone **Activity**

What causes air to enter and leave your lungs?

Materials

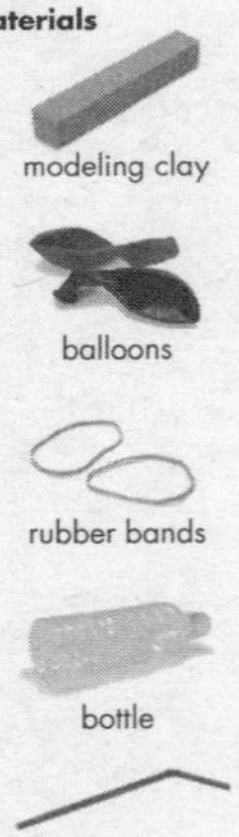

- modeling clay
- balloons
- rubber bands
- bottle
- straw

Process Skills

You can **make a model** of the lungs to see why air moves in and out.

What to Do

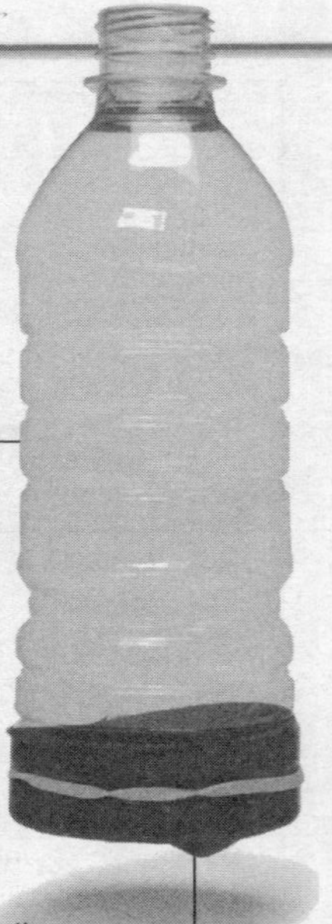

1. Stretch the open end of the red balloon over the cut end of the bottle. Twist the rubber band tightly around the bottle and the balloon.

2. Put the open end of the blue balloon over the end of the straw. Wrap the rubber band around the balloon and straw. Don't make the rubber band so tight that the straw gets crushed.

3. Push the balloon into the bottle through the hole in the bottle top. Seal the hole around the straw with clay.

4. Hold the model in one hand. With the other hand, pull the red balloon downward, away from the bottle. **Observe** and record what happens to the blue balloon.

5. Push the red balloon so that it reaches into the bottom of the bottle. Observe and record what happens to the blue balloon.

Explain Your Results

1. What happened to the blue balloon when you pulled on the red balloon? What happened when you pushed on the red balloon?
2. In the activity, which material **modeled** your lung? Which acted like the diaphragm that controls breathing?

Use with Chapter 5

10

Name ____________________

How can your fingers move?

❷–❹ Which fingers could you move without moving any other fingers? Record your **observations.**

	Observations
Step 2	
Step 3	
Step 4	

Explain Your Results

1. Describe your **observations.**

____

____

____

2. Did your **observations** surprise you? Explain.

____

____

____

Self-Assessment Checklist	
I followed instructions to move my fingers in the different situations.	______
I recorded my **observations.**	______
I described my **observations.**	______
I explained why my **observations** were or were not a surprise.	______

Notes for Home: Your child did an activity to **observe** how their fingers can move.
Home Activity: Have your child explain to you what they observed.

Name ______________________

Activity Flip Chart

Use with page 10

What causes air to enter and leave your lungs?

❹–❺ Pull the red balloon downward, away from the bottle. **Observe** and record what happens to the blue balloon. Push the red balloon so that it reaches into the bottom of the bottle. **Observe** and record what happens to the blue balloon.

	Observations
Red balloon pulled downward	
Red balloon pushed into bottle	

Explain Your Results

1. What happened to the blue balloon when you pulled on the red balloon? What happened when you pushed on the red balloon?

____

2. In the activity, which material **modeled** your lung? Which acted like the diaphragm that controls breathing?

____

____

Name ______________________________

Activity Flip Chart

Use with page 10

Self-Assessment Checklist	
I followed instructions to stretch the red balloon over the end of the bottle.	____
I followed instructions to attach the blue balloon to the straw.	____
I pulled the red balloon downward and recorded my **observations.**	____
I pushed the red balloon into the bottom of the bottle and recorded my **observations.**	____
I named the material that **modeled** a lung and the material that **modeled** a diaphragm.	____

Notes for Home: Your child did an activity to **make a model** of air entering and leaving the lungs.
Home Activity: With your child, **observe** the movement of your chest as you breathe before and after running.

Name ______________________________

Use with Unit A, pp. 172–175

Experiment: Do mealworms prefer damp or dry places?

Ask a question.

Do mealworms prefer to live in a damp place or a dry place?

State a hypothesis.

If mealworms can move to either a damp place or a dry place, then to which place will they move? Write your **hypothesis.**

____

____

Identify and control variables.

Identify each variable in the experiment.

independent variable ______________________________

dependent variable ______________________________

controlled variable ______________________________

Test your hypothesis. ❶–❻ Follow the steps to perform your experiment.

Collect and record your data.

	Number of Mealworms				
	Day 1	**Day 2**	**Day 3**	**Day 4**	**Day 5**
Damp Sponge					
Dry Sponge					

Interpret your data. Record your data in the bar graphs.

Mealworms Near Damp Sponge

10					
9					
8					
7					
6					
5					
4					
3					
2					
1					
	Day 1	**Day 2**	**Day 3**	**Day 4**	**Day 5**

Mealworms Near Dry Sponge

10					
9					
8					
7					
6					
5					
4					
3					
2					
1					
	Day 1	**Day 2**	**Day 3**	**Day 4**	**Day 5**

Name ______________________________

Use with Unit A, pp. 172–175

Compare what you see on the 2 graphs.

____

____

State your conclusion.
What conclusion can you draw from your graphs? Does it agree with your **hypothesis? Communicate** your conclusion.

____

____

Go Further
Mealworms are a young stage of a small beetle. Do the adult beetles prefer damp or dry places? Let the mealworms grow to be adults. Design and carry out a plan to investigate this or other questions you may have.

____

____

____

Self-Assessment Checklist	
I stated my **hypothesis** about where mealworms would choose to live.	____
I followed instructions to test my **hypothesis** and **observed** the results.	____
I **collected data** in a chart and **interpreted data** by making 2 bar graphs.	____
I compared what I saw on the 2 graphs.	____
I **communicated** my conclusion.	____

Notes for Home: Your child did an activity to **observe** how mealworms respond to changes in moisture in their surroundings.
Home Activity: With your child, name 3 other animals that would prefer a damp area to a dry area.

Explore: How can you make fresh water from salt water?

Explain Your Results

1. **Communicate:** What did you find in each container? Explain your results.

____

____

____

____

____

2. **Predict:** Think about the variables that affect evaporation. How could you speed up evaporation? Describe how you could test your prediction.

____

____

____

____

____

____

____

Name ______________________________

Use with Chapter 6, p. 180

Self-Assessment Checklist	
I followed instructions to make fresh water and let the water evaporate from the cup and bowl.	____
I **observed** the cups after 3 days.	____
I **communicated** my observations.	____
I **predicted** how I could speed up the evaporation.	____
I described how I could test my **prediction**.	____

Notes for Home: Your child did an activity to make fresh water out of salt water.
Home Activity: Have your child describe what happens to water that evaporates from the ocean.

Investigate: How does water change state?

1–5 Fill the cup with water up to the 30 mm mark on the ruler. Accurately record the height and temperature. Record the height and temperature for 4 more days.

	When Measurements Were Made						
	Day 1 Start	**Day 2** After freezing	**Day 2** When ice began to melt	**Day 2** When all ice was melted	**Day 3**	**Day 4**	**Day 5**
Height (mm)							
Temperature (°C)							

6 Make a bar graph showing how the height you **measured** changed.

Height of Ice and Liquid Water

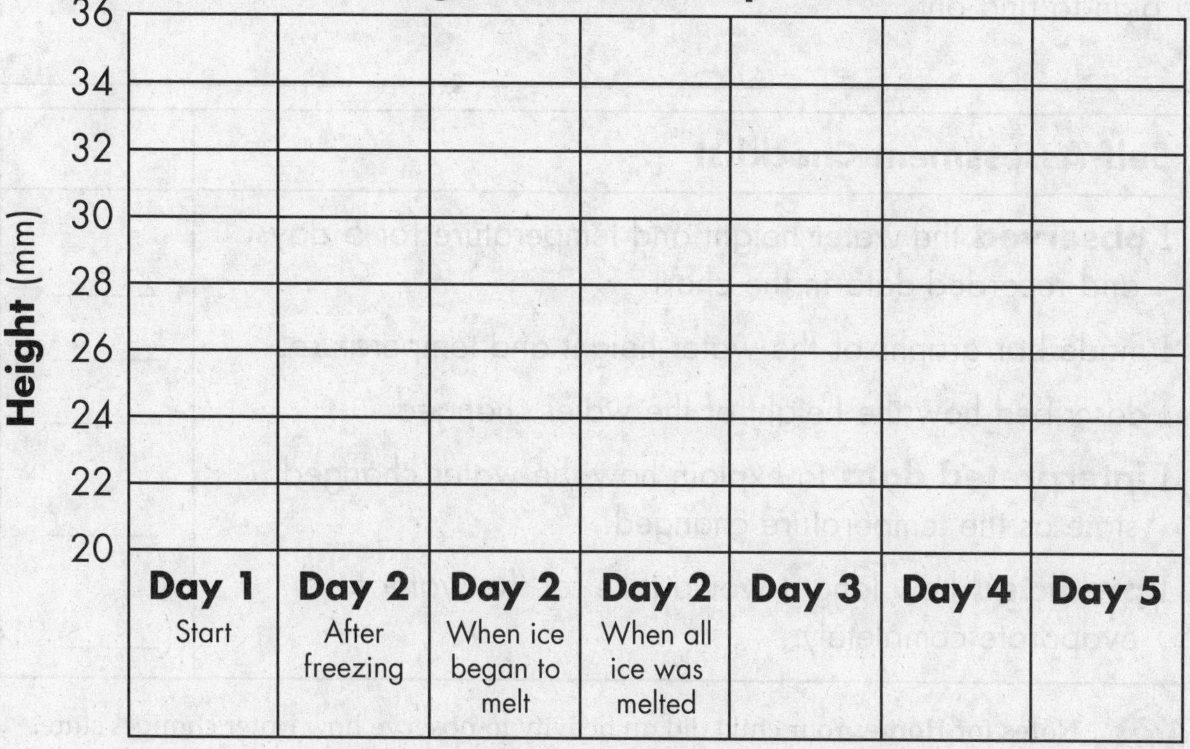

When Measurements Were Made

Explain Your Results

1. How did the height of the water change? Explain.

____

____

2. **Interpret Data:** As the temperature changed, what changes of state occurred? Was thermal energy added or removed during each change?

____

____

____

____

3. Based on your graph, **predict** how long it will take for the water to evaporate completely.

____

Go Further

What would happen if you added salt to the water before freezing? Make a plan to find out.

____

Self-Assessment Checklist	
I **observed** the water height and temperature for 5 days and recorded data in the chart.	______
I made bar graphs of the water height and temperature.	______
I described how the height of the water changed.	______
I **interpreted data** to explain how the water changed state as the temperature changed.	______
I **predicted** how long it would take for the water to evaporate completely.	______

Notes for Home: Your child did an activity to **observe** how water changes state.
Home Activity: With your child, discuss what conditions must exist for there to be snow.

Name ____________________

Use with Chapter 6

Lab zone **Activity**

Does air have mass?

Materials

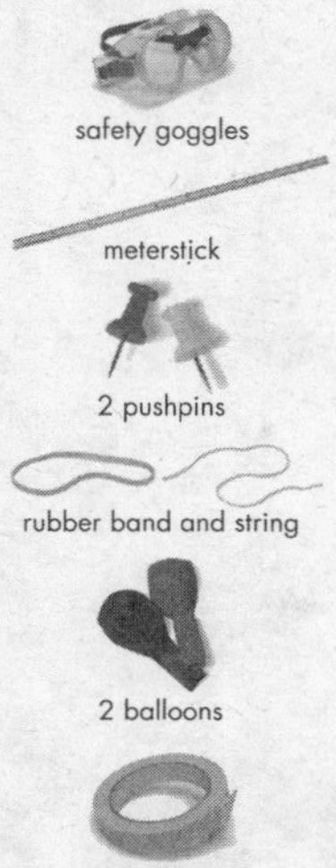

What to Do

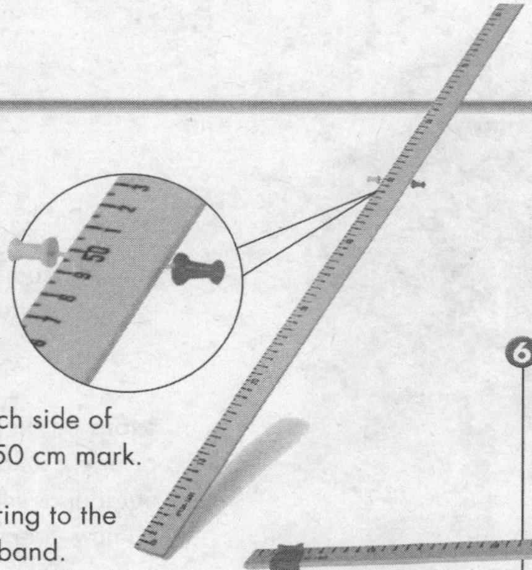

1. Put a pushpin into each side of the meterstick at the 50 cm mark.
2. Tie a long piece of string to the middle of the rubber band.
3. Place the two loops of the rubber band around the pushpins.

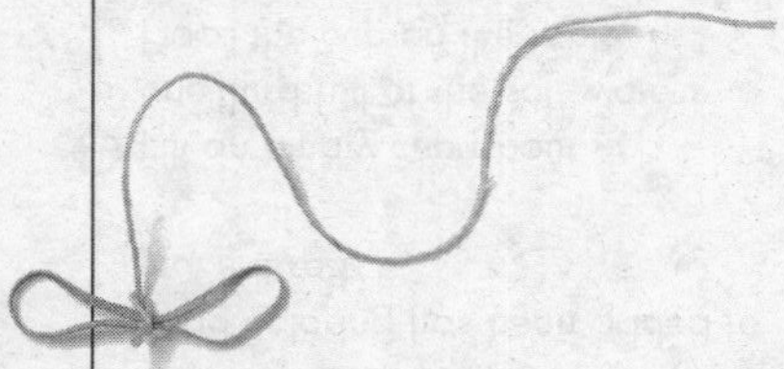

4. Lift the meterstick by the string. If the meterstick does not balance, move the pushpins until it does.
5. Tape one balloon to one end of the meterstick. Tape the second balloon to the other end. Check that the meterstick still balances. If it doesn't, move the balloons around until it balances.

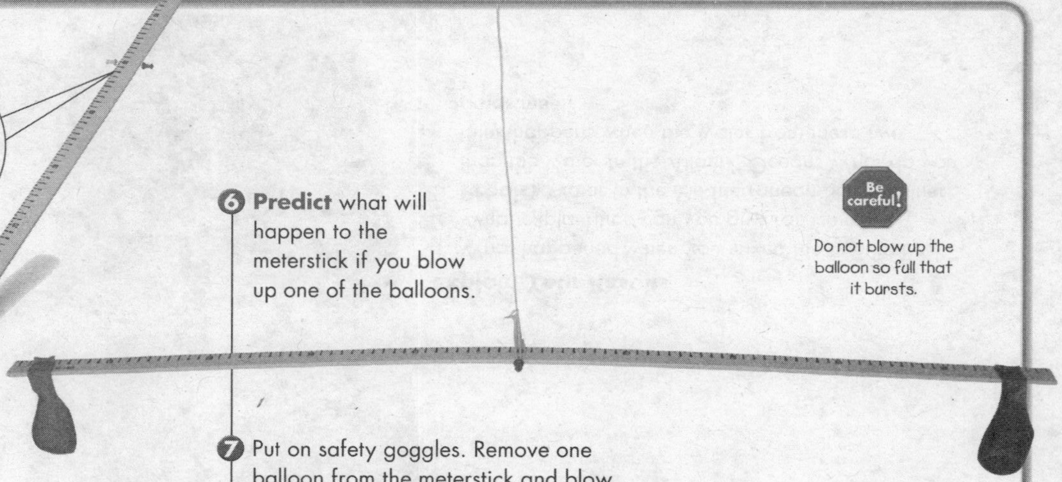

6. **Predict** what will happen to the meterstick if you blow up one of the balloons.

Be careful! Do not blow up the balloon so full that it bursts.

7. Put on safety goggles. Remove one balloon from the meterstick and blow it up. Leave enough at the end of the balloon to tie it shut. Tie the balloon shut with a short piece of string.
8. Tape the blown-up balloon to the end of the meterstick in the same place as before. **Observe** the meterstick and balloons. Record any changes you observe.

Process Skills

A **prediction** can be based on what you already know about air.

Explain Your Results

1. How did the balance of the meterstick change after one balloon was blown up?
2. **Infer** What caused the change?
3. **Predict** What would happen to the meterstick if you inflated the other balloon and taped it to the meterstick?

Use with Chapter 6

11

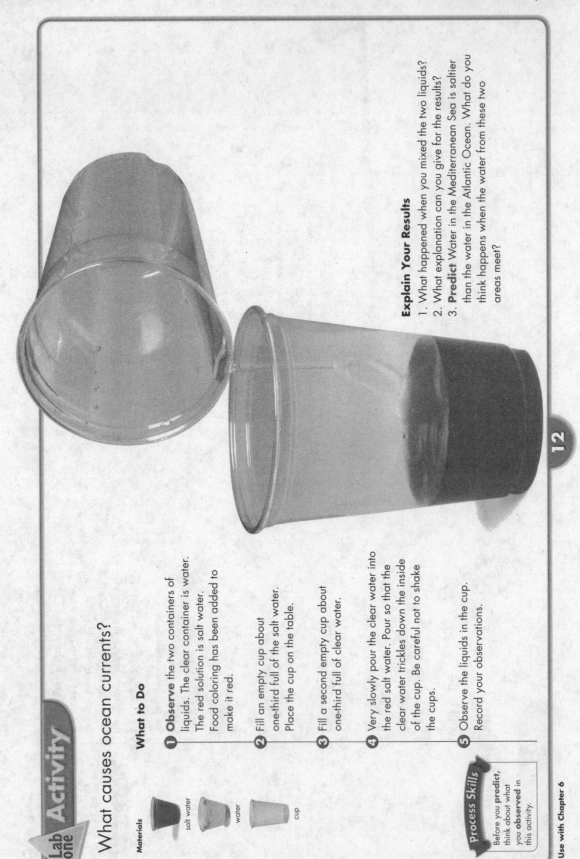

Lab zone Activity

What causes ocean currents?

Materials

What to Do

1. **Observe** the two containers of liquids. The clear container is water. The red solution is salt water. Food coloring has been added to make it red.
2. Fill an empty cup about one-third full of the salt water. Place the cup on the table.
3. Fill a second empty cup about one-third full of clear water.
4. Very slowly pour the clear water into the red salt water. Pour so that the clear water trickles down the inside of the cup. Be careful not to shake the cups.
5. Observe the liquids in the cup. Record your observations.

Process Skills

Before you **predict,** think about what you **observed** in this activity.

Explain Your Results

1. What happened when you mixed the two liquids?
2. What explanation can you give for the results?
3. **Predict** Water in the Mediterranean Sea is saltier than the water in the Atlantic Ocean. What do you think happens when the water from these two areas meet?

12

Use with Chapter 6

Name ______________________

Does air have mass?

Explain Your Results

1. How did the meterstick change after one balloon was blown up?

____

____

2. **Infer:** What caused the change?

____

____

3. **Predict:** What would happen to the meterstick if you inflated the other balloon and taped it to the meterstick?

____

____

____

____

Self-Assessment Checklist	
I followed instructions to prepare the meterstick and balance it on the string.	____
I balanced the meterstick with the balloons.	____
I blew up one of the balloons and **observed** and recorded the change.	____
I made an **inference** about what caused the change.	____
I **predicted** what would happen to the meterstick if I inflated the other balloon.	____

Notes for Home: Your child did an activity to observe that air has mass.
Home Activity: With your child, discuss what kind of particles make up air.

Name ____________________

Use with page 12

What causes ocean currents?

Explain Your Results

1. What happened when you mixed the two liquids?

2. What explanation can you give for the results?

3. Predict: Water in the Mediterranean Sea is saltier than the water in the Atlantic Ocean. What do you think happens when the water from these two areas meet?

Self-Assessment Checklist	
I **observed** the two containers of liquid.	____
I followed instructions to make a cup of red solution and a cup of clear water.	____
I poured the clear water into the red solution and recorded my **observations**.	____
I gave an explanation for my results.	____
I **predicted** what would happen when water from the Mediterranean Sea met ocean water.	____

Notes for Home: Your child did an activity to **observe** what causes ocean currents.
Home Activity: With your child, find and **observe** a map of the world's ocean currents.

Name ____________________

Lab zone **Directed Inquiry**

Use with Chapter 7, p. 212

Explore: How can you make a model of a hurricane?

Explain Your Results

Compare and contrast your model and a real hurricane.

____

____

____

____

Self-Assessment Checklist	
I followed instructions to **make a model** of a hurricane.	______
I put newspaper on the table.	______
I stirred water in a bowl and added food coloring to the center.	______
I watched the food coloring make a spiral.	______
I compared and contrasted my model and a real hurricane.	______

Notes for Home: Your child did an activity to make a model of a hurricane.
Home Activity: With your child, conduct research to determine what weather conditions cause a hurricane.

Name ______________________________

Lab zone **Guided Inquiry**

Use with Chapter 7, pp. 226–227

Investigate: Where is the hurricane going?

❶ **Predict** where the hurricane will go next. Record your **prediction** in the Predictions Chart.

Predictions Chart

Step	**Prediction** What places would you warn that a hurricane might be approaching?	**Accuracy** How accurate was your prediction?
1st prediction (Step 1)		
2nd prediction (Step 2)		

❷ Mark the position of the hurricane on day 3. Make a new **prediction.** Predict where the hurricane will go next. What places would you warn? Record your **prediction** in the chart.

❸ Mark where the hurricane was on day 4 and day 5. Complete the Predictions Chart.

Explain Your Results

1. How did you **predict** where the hurricane might go?

____

____

2. How might people be affected by an accurate **prediction?** by a **prediction** that is not accurate?

____

____

____

____

Name ________________________________

Go Further

Hurricanes are a type of severe weather. Think about the weather in your area. How could you track the weather in your area over the course of three weeks? Make and carry out a plan. Decide what weather data you will collect and what weather tools you will need.

____

____

____

Self-Assessment Checklist	
I followed instructions to **observe** the path of the hurricane on the storm map.	____
I **predicted** where the hurricane would go and recorded my **predictions** in the chart.	____
I marked the position of the hurricane on day 3, day 4, and day 5.	____
I explained how I **predicted** the path of the hurricane.	____
I determined how people might be affected by an accurate **prediction** and by a **prediction** that is not accurate.	____

Notes for Home: Your child did an activity to **predict** the path of a hurricane.
Home Activity: With your child, **observe** the weather report in the newspaper or on television and identify any hurricanes.

Name ____________________

Lab zone **Activity**

How do winds cause waves?

Materials

pan

water

metric ruler

drinking straw

What to Do

1. Fill the pan with about 1 cm of water. Let the water sit until it becomes still.
2. Place the straw at an angle above the center of the pan. Blow through the straw onto the top of the water. **Observe** the size of the waves. Record your observations.
3. Wait until the water becomes still. Blow across the top of the water again but over a longer distance. Does the size of the waves differ from those in step 2? Record your observations.

4. Again wait until the water becomes still. Aim the straw directly down at the center of the pan. Gently blow one puff of air through the straw onto the top of the water. Observe the waves. Record your observations.

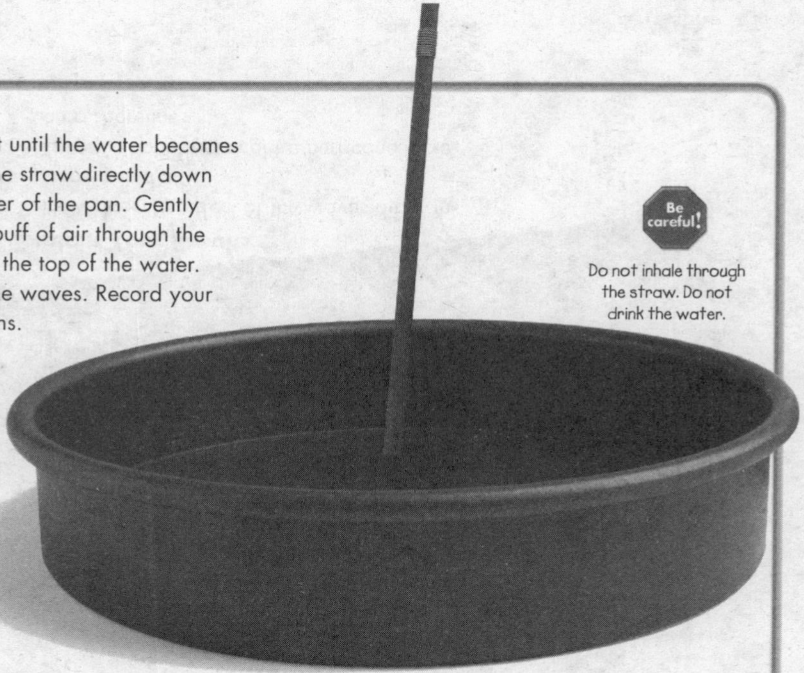

Be careful! Do not inhale through the straw. Do not drink the water.

5. Wait until the water becomes still. Then blow a harder puff of air through the straw. How do the waves compare to those in step 4? Record your observations.

Process Skills

You can **communicate** your ideas about wind and waves by thinking about what you **observed.**

Explain Your Results

1. In step 3, how did the size of the waves compare to those in step 2?
2. Compare the waves in step 4 with those in step 5.
3. **Communicate** Write a paragraph that explains how wind affects the size of waves.

Lab zone Activity

How do waves cause shore erosion?

Materials

sand

water

fish tank

What to Do

1. Mix a little water into the sand in the bucket until the sand sticks together.
2. Pack the sand into a slope at one end of the fish tank.
3. Pour water into the empty end of the tank until it is about two-thirds as deep as the sand. Pour the water carefully so that you don't disturb the sand.
4. **Model** Use your hand to make gentle waves in the water. The gentle waves represent ocean waves during normal weather. **Observe** the waves' effects on the sand. Record your observations.
5. Make much stronger waves in the water. These waves represent ocean waves during a hurricane. Observe and record what happens to the sand.

Process Skills

Before you make an **inference,** think about what you have **observed.**

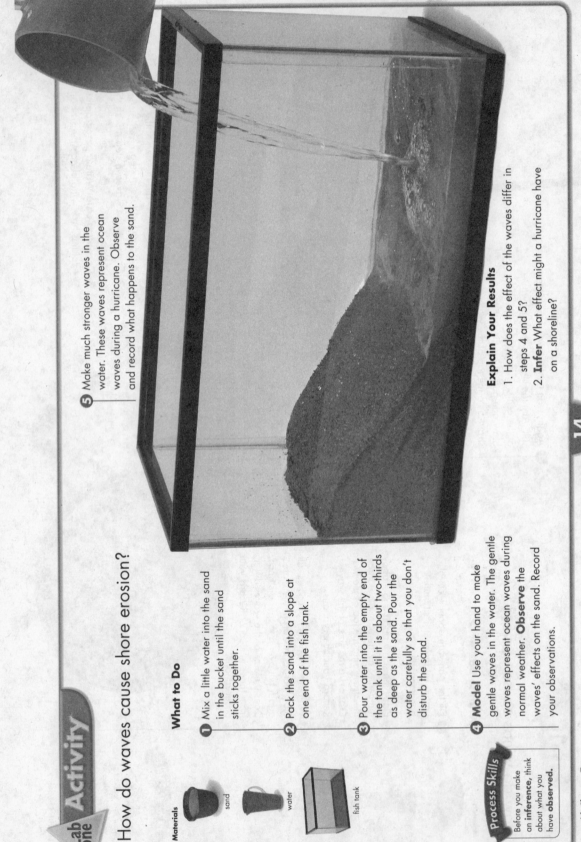

Explain Your Results

1. How does the effect of the waves differ in steps 4 and 5?
2. **Infer** What effect might a hurricane have on a shoreline?

Use with Chapter 7

14

Name ______________________

Use with page 13

How do winds cause waves?

❷–❺ Place the straw at an angle above the center of the pan. Blow through the straw onto the top of the water. **Observe** the size of the waves. Record your observations. Blow across the top of the water again but over a longer distance. Does the size of the waves differ from those in step 2? Record your observations. Aim the straw directly down at the center of the pan. Gently blow one puff of air through the straw onto the water. Observe the waves. Record your observations. Blow a puff of air harder through the straw. How do the waves compare to those in step 4? Record your observations.

Location of Straw	Observations
at angle above center	
at angle above center, longer distance	
directly down center of pan	
directly down center of pan, harder puff	

Explain Your Results

1. In step 3, how did the size of the waves compare to those in step 2?

____

2. Compare the waves in step 4 with those in step 5.

____

____

Name ______________________

Use with page 13

3. Communicate: Write a paragraph that explains how wind affects the size of waves.

____

____

____

____

____

Self-Assessment Checklist	
I placed the straw at an angle above the center of the pan, blew, and recorded my **observations**.	____
I blew across the water again for a longer distance and recorded my **observations**.	____
I aimed the straw down the center, blew gently and then hard, and recorded my **observations**.	____
I compared the waves in step 3 with those in step 2, and those in step 4 with those in step 5.	____
I **communicated** how wind affects the size of waves in a paragraph.	____

Notes for Home: Your child did an activity to **observe** how wind causes waves.
Home Activity: With your child, **observe** the wave pattern when you toss a coin into a bowl of water at different points.

Name ______________________________

Use with page 14

How do waves cause shore erosion?

4 **Model:** Use your hand to make gentle waves in the water. The gentle waves represent ocean waves during normal weather. **Observe** the waves' effects on the sand. Record your observations.

____

____

5 Make stronger waves in the water. These waves represent ocean waves during a hurricane. Observe and record what happens to the sand.

____

____

Explain Your Results

1. How does the effect of waves differ in steps 4 and 5?

____

____

2. Infer: What effect might a hurricane have on a shoreline?

____

____

Name ___________________________________

Self-Assessment Checklist	
I followed instructions to make a slope of sand in the fish tank and to add water.	____
I used my hand to **model** ocean waves during normal weather and recorded my **observations**.	____
I **observed** and recorded what happened to the sand when I made stronger waves.	____
I described how the effect of the waves differed in steps 4 and 5.	____
I made an **inference** about the effect a hurricane might have on a shoreline.	____

Notes for Home: Your child did an activity to **model** how waves cause shoreline erosion.
Home Activity: With your child, find and **observe** pictures of beach erosion after a hurricane.

Name ______________________

Use with Chapter 8, p. 236

Explore: How can you classify rocks and minerals?

1. **Observe** the rock and mineral samples. Examine them with a hand lens. Record your observations.

   Sample #1: ______________________

   Sample #2: ______________________

   Sample #3: ______________________

   Sample #4: ______________________

   Sample #5: ______________________

   Sample #6: ______________________

   Sample #7: ______________________

   Sample #8: ______________________

2. Tell how the samples are alike and different. List words you could use to describe and sort your samples.

   ____

   ____

   ____

   ____

Explain Your Results

How did you **classify** the samples?

____

____

Name ______________________________

Directed Inquiry

Use with Chapter 8, p. 236

Self-Assessment Checklist	
I **observed** the rock and mineral samples.	______
I thought of ways to describe the rock and mineral samples.	______
I determined how the samples are like each other and how they differ.	______
I listed words that could be used to describe and sort the samples.	______
I **classified** the samples into 2 to 4 groups.	______

Notes for Home: Your child did an activity about classifying rocks and minerals.
Home Activity: Have your child explain to you why different rocks look different.

Name ____________________ Lab zone **Guided Inquiry**

Use with Chapter 8, pp. 250–251

Investigate: What properties can you use to identify minerals?

2–5 Record the color and luster of each mineral in your Table of Observed Properties. Rub each mineral across a streak plate. Record the color of the streak. Identify your minerals.

Table of Observed Properties

Mineral	Observed Properties				Identity of Mineral
	Color	Luster (glassy or metallic)	Streak	Hardness	
Mineral A				6	
Mineral B				not measured	
Mineral C				not measured	
Mineral D				not measured	
Mineral E				not measured	
Mineral F				2.5	

Name ________________________________

Lab zone **Guided Inquiry**

Use with Chapter 8, pp. 250–251

Explain Your Results

1. What is Mineral E? What were its properties that you **observed?**

____

____

2. What properties did you use to describe and identify the minerals?

____

____

Go Further

How could you test the hardness of the materials by scratching them with different objects? Make a plan to investigate this or other questions about minerals.

____

____

____

Self-Assessment Checklist	
I **observed** the properties of each mineral using a hand lens.	____
I recorded the color, luster, and streak color of each mineral in the Table of Observed Properties.	____
I scratched Mineral A against Mineral F and compared my results to the numbers on the chart.	____
I identified the minerals.	____
I listed the properties I used to describe and identify the minerals.	____

Notes for Home: Your child did an activity to identify minerals.
Home Activity: With your child, **observe** and identify rocks and minerals found in your local environment.

Lab zone **Activity**

How do rocks form?

Materials

clay

What to Do

1. **Model** the rock cycle. Begin by forming the clay into tiny balls.

2. Gather the clay balls together in a pile. Lightly press on the clay just until the balls stick together. **Observe** and record how the balls differ from the way they were in step 1.

3. Press down harder on the clay to flatten the balls. Fold the clay in half and press down again. Record how the clay looks.

4. Knead the clay until it becomes one color. How has the temperature of the clay changed? Record your observations.

5. Form the clay into a ball. Break off bits of clay to form several smaller balls.

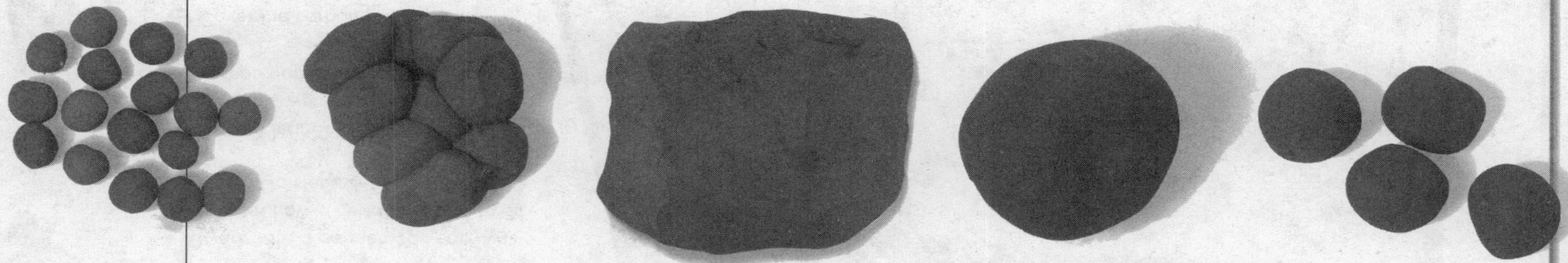

Process Skills

You can **classify** objects according to what you **observe.**

Explain Your Results

1. What process of the rock cycle did you **model** in step 2?
2. **Classify** What type of rock did you make in step 3? In step 4?
3. **Communicate** Use your model to describe the rock cycle.

15

Name ____________________

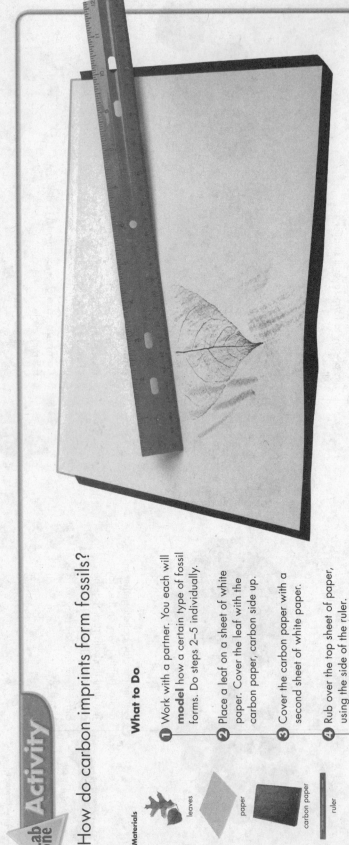

Lab zone **Activity**

How do carbon imprints form fossils?

Materials

What to Do

1. Work with a partner. You each will **model** how a certain type of fossil forms. Do steps 2–5 individually.
2. Place a leaf on a sheet of white paper. Cover the leaf with the carbon paper, carbon side up.
3. Cover the carbon paper with a second sheet of white paper.
4. Rub over the top sheet of paper, using the side of the ruler.
5. Remove the top sheet of paper. Observe the imprint on the bottom side of the paper.
6. **Infer** Exchange rubbings with your partner. Using the rubbing, write a description of what you think your partner's leaf looks like. Then compare your description to the actual leaf.

Process Skills

Making a **model** can help you **infer** how fossils form.

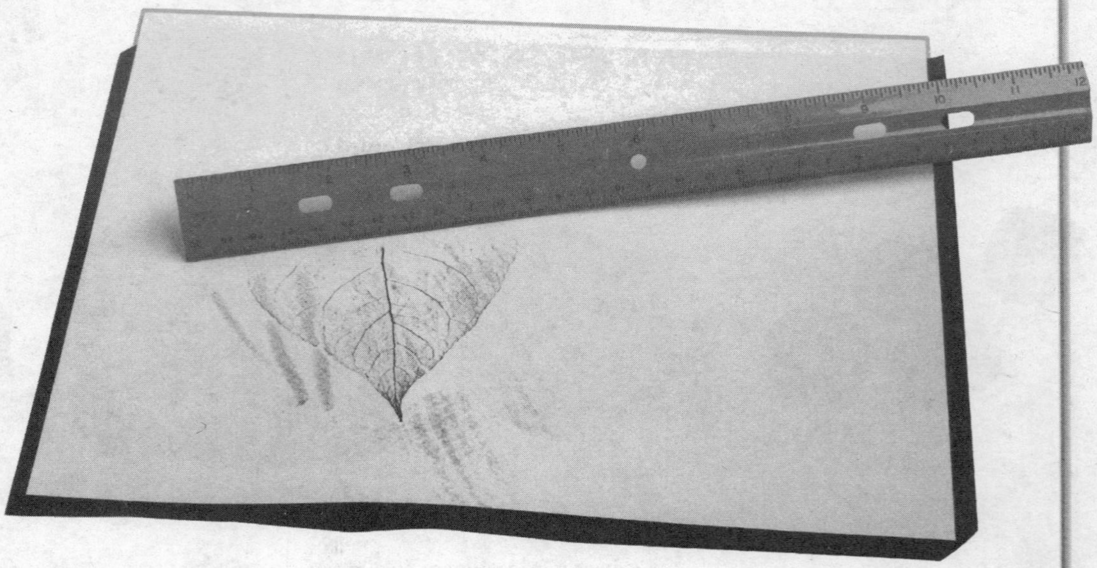

Explain Your Results

1. What parts of the leaf could you see on your partner's rubbing?
2. What could you **infer** about your partner's leaf from the rubbing? What couldn't you infer?
3. The type of fossil you modeled was a carbon imprint. This kind of fossil forms when a plant dies and leaves behind a thin layer of carbon when it decays. The carbon layer shows some of the features of the plant. How is your **model** similar to a carbon impression? How is it different?

Use with Chapter 8

16

Name ______________________________

Activity Flip Chart

Use with page 15

How do rocks form?

❷–❹ Gather the balls of clay together in a pile. Lightly press on the pile of clay just until the balls stick together. **Observe** and record how the balls differ from the way they were in step 1. Press down harder on the clay to flatten the balls. Fold the clay in half and press down again. Record how the clay looks. Knead the clay until it becomes one color. How has the temperature of the clay changed? Record your observations.

Form of the Clay	Observations
after piling clay and pressing	
after balls have been flattened and the clay folded in half	
after kneading the clay	

Explain Your Results

1. What process of the rock cycle did you **model** in step 2?

____

2. Classify: What type of rock did you make in step 3? In step 4?

____

____

____

3. Communicate: Use your model to describe the rock cycle.

____

____

Name ______________________________

Use with page 15

Self-Assessment Checklist	
I made a **model** of a group of rocks by forming clay into tiny balls.	____
I followed instructions to change the form of the clay and recorded my **observations.**	____
I named the process of the rock cycle that I **modeled** in step 2.	____
I **classified** the rock produced in step 3 and step 4.	____
I **communicated** a description of the rock cycle with the aid of my **model.**	____

Notes for Home: Your child did an activity to **model** the process by which rock forms.
Home Activity: Have your child explain to you what kinds of rock are layered inside the Earth.

Name ________________________________

How do carbon imprints form in fossils?

6 **Infer:** Exchange rubbings with your partner. Using the rubbing, write a description of what you think your partner's leaf looked like.

____

____

Explain Your Results

1. What parts of the leaf could you see on your partner's rubbing?

____

____

2. What could you **infer** about the leaf from the rubbing? What couldn't you infer?

____

____

____

3. The type of fossil you modeled was a carbon imprint. This kind of fossil forms when a plant dies and leaves behind a thin layer of carbon when it decays. The carbon layer shows some of the features of the plant. How is your **model** similar to a carbon impression? How is it different?

____

____

____

Name ______________________

Activity Flip Chart

Use with page 16

Self-Assessment Checklist	
I followed instructions to **make a model** of a carbon imprint of a leaf.	____
I made an **inference** about what my partner's leaf looked like.	____
I named the parts of the leaf I could see on my partner's rubbing.	____
I explained what **inferences** could and could not be made about the leaf from the rubbing.	____
I described how my **model** is similar to and different from a carbon impression.	____

Notes for Home: Your child did an activity to **make a model** of how carbon imprints form in fossils.
Home Activity: With your child, name 3 organisms that would be likely to show up in these kinds of fossils.

Name ________________________________ Lab zone **Directed Inquiry**

Use with Chapter 9, p. 260

Explore: How can you observe a mineral wear away?

1. Shake chalk and rocks in a jar for 1 minute. Look for changes in the chalk. Shake for 3 minutes more. **Observe** the chalk. Write your **observations.**

____

____

2. Empty out the jar. Fill the jar $\frac{1}{2}$ full of water. Repeat step 1 using the rocks, 4 new pieces of chalk, and water. Write your **observations.**

____

____

Explain Your Results

1. How did the chalk change after being shaken with rocks for 1 minute? For 3 minutes?

____

____

____

____

2. Infer: Compared to shaking chalk with only rocks, what effect did shaking chalk with both rocks and water have on the chalk?

____

____

____

____

Self-Assessment Checklist	
I followed instructions to prepare the 2 jars.	______
I **observed** what happened after I shook the jars.	______
I wrote my **observations**.	______
I described how the chalk changed after being shaken with rocks for 1 minute and 3 minutes.	______
I made an **inference** about the effect of shaking chalk with rocks and water.	______

Notes for Home: Your child made a model to represent the effect of water and rocks on the weathering of substances.
Home Activity: With your child, list 3 ways that rocks at a waterfall are affected by weather.

Name ________________________________ Lab zone **Guided Inquiry**

Use with Chapter 9, pp. 274–275

Investigate: How does distance change earthquake effects?

❸ Tap at the specified location for 30 seconds. **Observe** what happens to the popcorn at each location. Record your observations in the chart.

Location	What happened to the popcorn?
Location A (nearest epicenter)	
Location B	
Location C (farthest from the epicenter)	

Explain Your Results

1. Infer: Why do you think the popcorn at different locations moved different amounts?

____

____

2. How would knowing where earthquakes might occur help you decide where to put a building?

____

____

Name ______________________________

Use with Chapter 9, pp. 274–275

Go Further

Does how long an earthquake lasts change its effects? Make a plan to investigate this question or one of your own.

____

____

____

Self-Assessment Checklist	
I followed instructions to prepare a box with popcorn on each end and in the center.	____
I tapped the box and **observed** what happened to the popcorn.	____
I recorded my **observations** in the chart.	____
I made an **inference** about why popcorn at different locations moved different amounts.	____
I **inferred** how knowing where earthquakes might occur would help me decide where to put a building.	____

Notes for Home: Your child did an activity to **observe** how earthquake severity is affected by distance from the epicenter.
Home Activity: With your child, discuss steps you can take to be prepared for an earthquake.

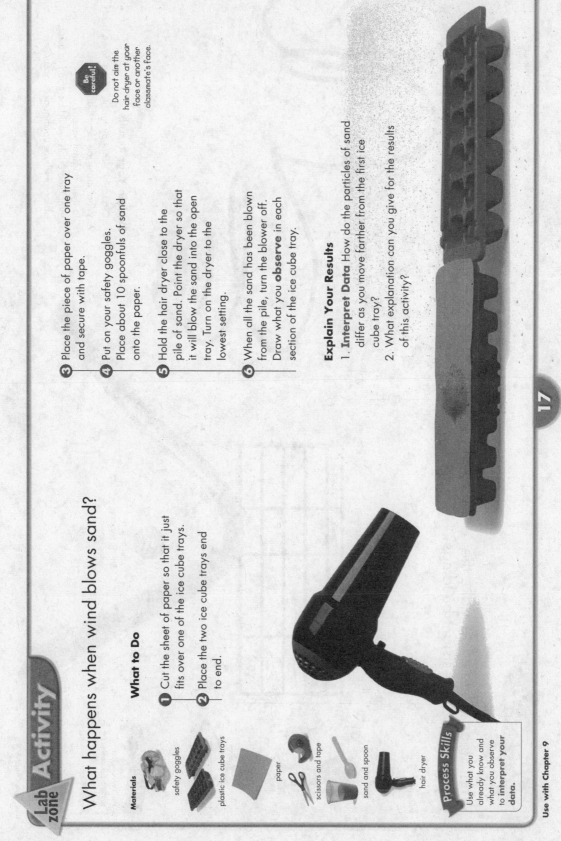

Lab zone **Activity**

What happens when wind blows sand?

Materials

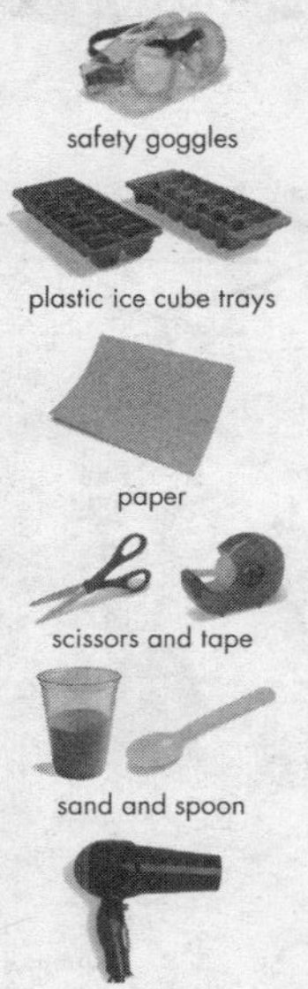

safety goggles
plastic ice cube trays
paper
scissors and tape
sand and spoon
hair dryer

Process Skills

Use what you already know and what you observe to **interpret your data.**

What to Do

1. Cut the sheet of paper so that it just fits over one of the ice cube trays.
2. Place the two ice cube trays end to end.
3. Place the piece of paper over one tray and secure with tape.
4. Put on your safety goggles. Place about 10 spoonfuls of sand onto the paper.
5. Hold the hair dryer close to the pile of sand. Point the dryer so that it will blow the sand into the open tray. Turn on the dryer to the lowest setting.
6. When all the sand has been blown from the pile, turn the blower off. Draw what you **observe** in each section of the ice cube tray.

Be careful! Do not aim the hair dryer at your face or another classmate's face.

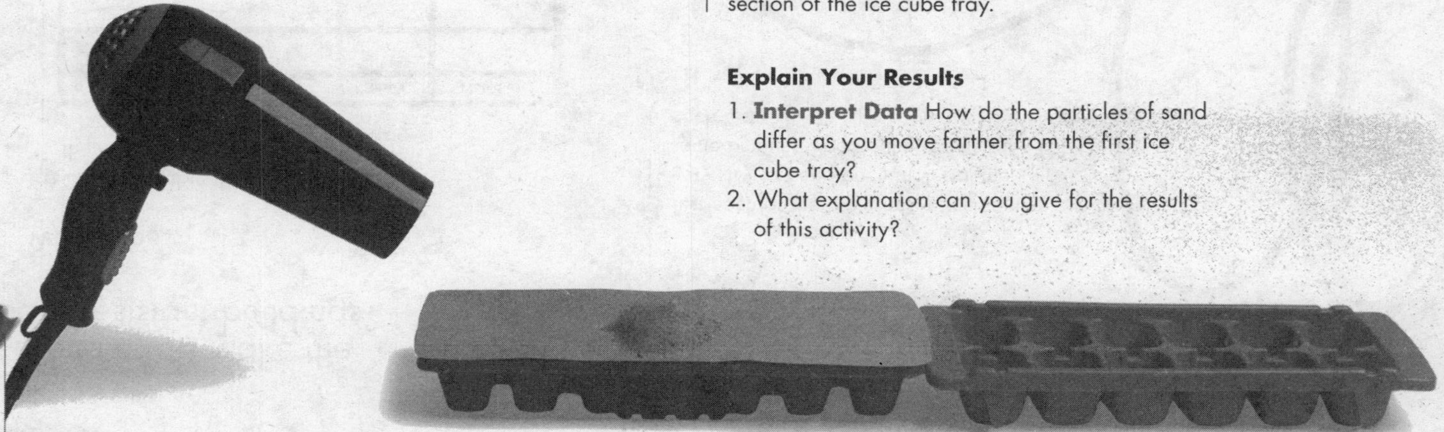

Explain Your Results

1. **Interpret Data** How do the particles of sand differ as you move farther from the first ice cube tray?
2. What explanation can you give for the results of this activity?

Use with Chapter 9

17

Lab zone **Activity**

What kinds of materials make the best earthquake-resistant buildings?

Materials

safety goggles

gloves

paper

building materials

What to Do

1. Copy the table. Record the names of the materials you are testing.

Material	How far bent	Result	Would use

2. **Collect Data** Choose one material and bend it slightly. Record how far you bent it and what happens, such as whether it broke, stayed bent, or returned to its original shape.

3. Test each of the materials in the same way. Try to bend each material the same amount. Record the results for each test.

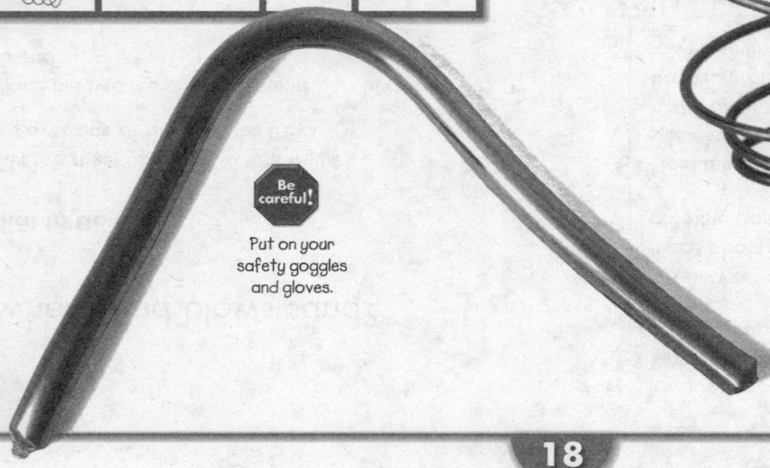

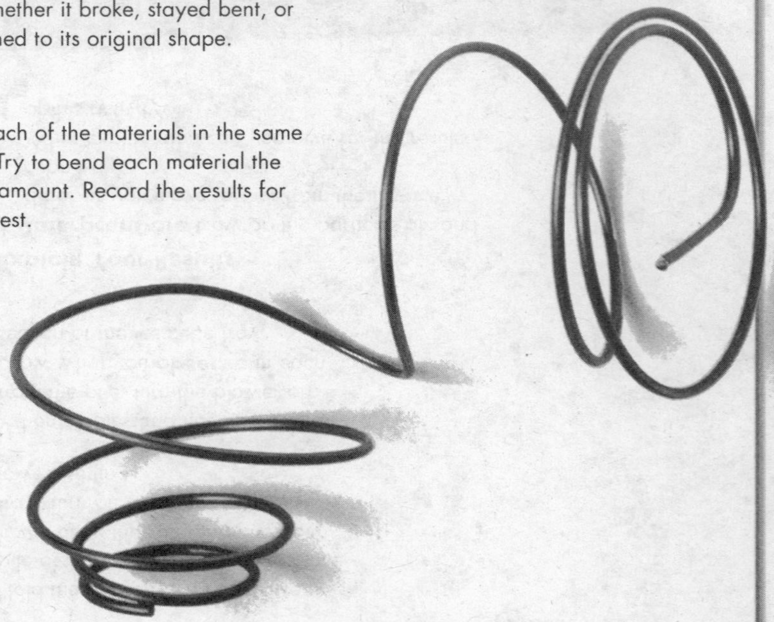

Be careful! Put on your safety goggles and gloves.

Process Skills

You can use the **data you collect** to **classify** things into different groups, according to their similarities and differences.

Explain Your Results

1. **Classify** What materials broke when bent?
2. What materials bent then returned to their original shape?
3. What materials would be good to use in an area where earthquakes occur?

Use with Chapter 9

18

Name ______________________________

Use with page 17

What happens when wind blows sand?

6 When all the sand has been blown from the pile, turn the blower off. Draw what you observe in each of the ice cube tray boxes.

Explain Your Results

1. **Interpret Data:** How do the particles of sand differ as you move farther from the first ice cube tray?

____

____

____

2. What explanation can you give for the results of this activity?

____

____

Name ______________________

Use with page 17

Self-Assessment Checklist	
I followed instructions to set up the ice cube trays and the sand.	____
I followed instructions to blow the sand into the open tray with the hairdryer.	____
I drew what I **observed** in each of the ice cube tray boxes.	____
I **interpreted my data** to describe how the particles of sand differ farther from the first tray.	____
I explained the results of the activity.	____

Notes for Home: Your child did an activity to examine what happens when wind blows sand.
Home Activity: With your child, name 2 other effects wind can have on the landscape.

Name ______________________________

What kinds of materials make the best earthquake-resistant buildings?

❶–❸ Copy the table. Record the names of the materials you are testing. **Collect Data:** Choose one material and bend it slightly. Record how far you bent it and what happened, such as whether it broke, stayed bent, or returned to its original shape. Test each of the materials the same way. Try to bend each material the same amount. Record the results for each test.

Name ______________________________

Use with page 18

Explain Your Results

1. Classify: What material broke when bent?

____

____

2. What materials bent then returned to their original shape?

____

____

____

____

3. What materials would be good to use in an area where earthquakes occur?

____

Self-Assessment Checklist	
I copied the table and recorded the names of the materials to be tested.	____
I tested the materials by bending them and recorded the results.	____
I described what material broke when bent.	____
I listed the materials that bent and then returned to their original shape.	____
I named the materials that would be good to use in an area where earthquakes occur.	____

Notes for Home: Your child did an activity to determine what kinds of materials make the best earthquake-resistant buildings.
Home Activity: With your child, discuss how you would design a building that would minimize damages and casualties in a tornado.

Name ______________________

Lab zone **Directed Inquiry**

Use with Chapter 10, p. 284

Explore: How can you collect sunlight?

③ **Measure** and record the temperatures after 1 minute and after 3 minutes.

Temperatures after 1 minute: ______________________

Temperatures after 3 minutes: ______________________

Explain Your Results

1. Compare the effects of sunlight on the two thermometers.

____

____

2. Infer: What caused the temperatures to be different?

____

____

____

Self-Assessment Checklist	
I followed instructions to make a solar collector.	____
I **measured** the temperatures after 1 minute and after 3 minutes.	____
I recorded my measurements.	____
I compared the effects of sunlight on the 2 thermometers.	____
I **inferred** about what caused the temperatures to be different.	____

Notes for Home: Your child did an activity to make and test a solar collector.
Home Activity: With your child, discuss how a solar collector could be used to provide heat to a house.

Name ______________________________

Guided Inquiry

Use with Chapter 10, pp. 298–299

Investigate: How can you observe a "fossil fuel" being formed?

5 Put the bottle in a warm place for 5 days. Each day **observe** the balloon and the contents of the bottle. Try to detect *any* change. Record on your chart what you observe.

Day	Balloon	Contents of Bottle
Day 1		
Day 2		
Day 3		
Day 4		
Day 5		

Explain Your Results

1. Did the balloon and the contents of the bottle change? How?

____

____

2. **Infer:** What made the balloon change?

____

____

Go Further

What would happen to the formation of natural gas if you changed the conditions, such as the temperature or the amount of water? Make a plan to find out.

____

____

____

Self-Assessment Checklist	
I followed instructions to **make a model.**	_____
I **observed** how the balloon and the contents of the bottle changed.	_____
I recorded my **observations** in the chart.	_____
I described the changes I **observed.**	_____
I **made an inference** about what made the balloon change.	_____

Notes for Home: Your child did an activity to **make a model** of how fossil fuels form.
Home Activity: With your child, discuss what kind of fuel provides energy and heat for your home.

Lab zone **Activity**

How do particles of soil differ?

Materials

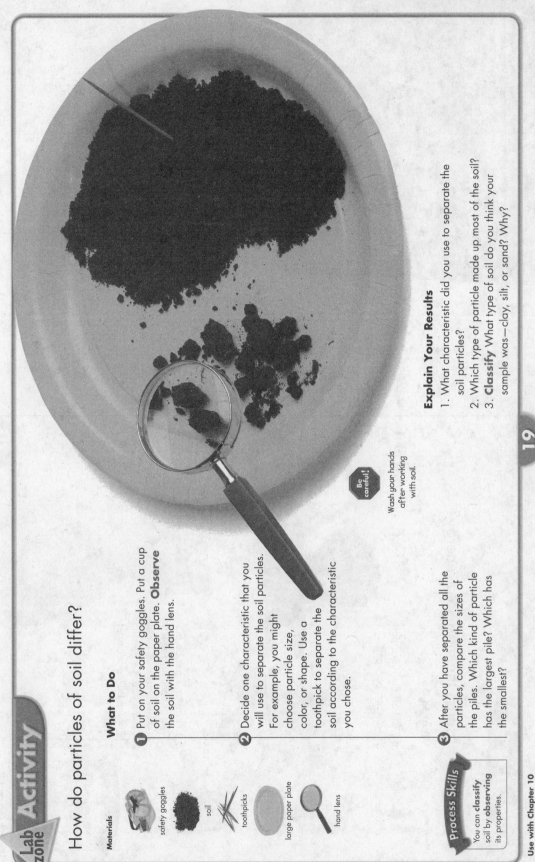

- safety goggles
- soil
- toothpicks
- large paper plate
- hand lens

You can **classify** soil by **observing** its properties.

What to Do

1. Put on your safety goggles. Put a cup of soil on the paper plate. **Observe** the soil with the hand lens.
2. Decide one characteristic that you will use to separate the soil particles. For example, you might choose particle size, color, or shape. Use a toothpick to separate the soil according to the characteristic you chose.
3. After you have separated all the particles, compare the sizes of the piles. Which kind of particle has the largest pile? Which has the smallest?

Be careful! Wash your hands after working with soil.

Explain Your Results

1. What characteristic did you use to separate the soil particles?
2. Which type of particle made up most of the soil?
3. **Classify** What type of soil do you think your sample was—clay, silt, or sand? Why?

Use with Chapter 10

19

Lab zone **Activity**

What color absorbs the most solar energy?

Materials

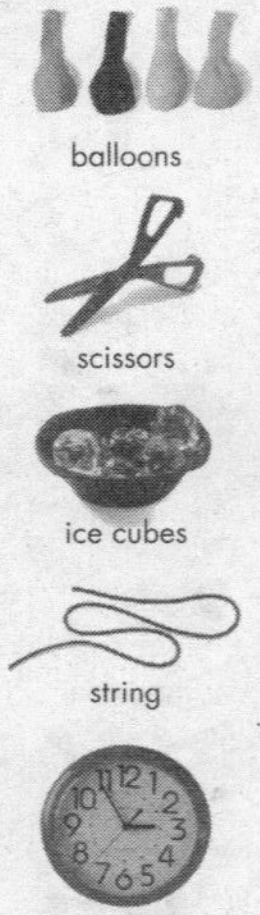

What to Do

1. Cut off the rolled part of each balloon.

2. Place an ice cube in each balloon. The ice cubes should all be the same size. Tie the ends of the balloons closed with string.

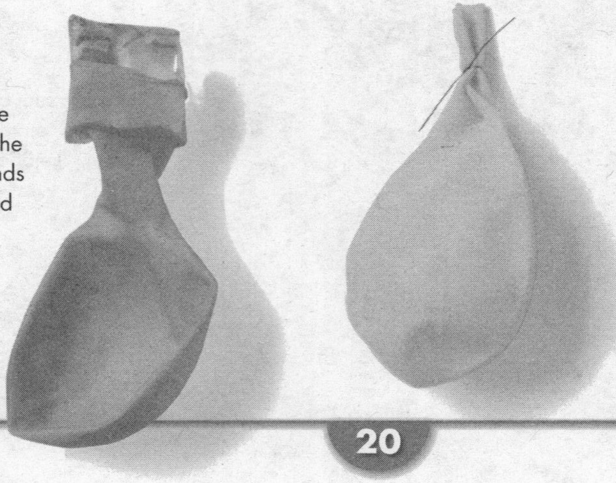

3. Place the balloons in direct sunlight. Place them with the opening upward. **Predict** which ice cube will melt first. Record your prediction.

4. Check the balloons every 3 minutes. Pinch the balloons to see if the ice has melted. Record the time it takes for the ice cube in each balloon to melt completely.

Explain Your Results

1. In which balloon did the ice melt first? Was your prediction correct?
2. Why do you think the ice melted faster in some balloons than in others?
3. **Infer** If you wanted to stay cool in hot weather, what color clothing would be best—white or black?

Process Skills

When you **predict** which ice cube will melt first, think about what you already know about solar energy.

Use with Chapter 10

20

Name ______________________

Use with page 19

What materials can be found in soil?

3. After you have separated all of the particles, compare the sizes of the piles. Which kind of particle has the largest pile? Which has the smallest?

____

____

Explain Your Results

1. What characteristic did you use to separate the soil particles?

____

____

2. Which type of particle made up most of the soil?

____

____

3. **Classify:** What type of soil do you think your sample was—clay, silt, or sand? Why?

____

____

Name ______________________

Self-Assessment Checklist	
I **observed** the soil and decided on a characteristic to use to separate the particles.	____
I separated the different particles into piles and compared the sizes of the piles.	____
I named the characteristic I used to separate the soil particles.	____
I described the type of particle that made up most of the soil.	____
I **classified** my soil and explained why I chose that classification.	____

Notes for Home: Your child did an activity to **observe** and **classify** the materials found in soil.
Home Activity: With your child, compare the soil in your community to the soil studied in class.

What color absorbs the most solar energy?

3. Place the balloons in direct sunlight. Place them with the opening upward. **Predict** which ice cube will melt first. Record your prediction.

____

4. Check the balloons every 3 minutes. Pinch the balloons to see if the ice has melted. Record the time it takes for the ice cube in each balloon to melt completely.

Color of Balloon	Time It Takes for Ice Cube to Melt Completely

Explain Your Results

1. In which balloon did the ice melt first? Was your prediction correct?

____

____

2. Why do you think the ice melted faster in some balloons than in others?

____

____

Name ______________________________

3. Infer: If you wanted to stay cool in hot weather, what color clothing would be best—white or black?

____

Self-Assessment Checklist	
I followed instructions to put the ice cubes inside the balloons and put the balloons in sunlight.	____
I **predicted** which ice cube would melt first.	____
I recorded the time it took for the ice in each balloon to melt completely.	____
I described why the ice melted faster in some balloons than in others.	____
I made an **inference** about what color clothing would be best to stay cool in hot weather.	____

Notes for Home: Your child did an activity to determine what color absorbs the most solar energy.
Home Activity: With your child, discuss how the information learned in the activity could be used to design an energy-efficient home.

Name ______________________

Use with Unit B, pp. 308–311

Experiment: What affects how rain erodes soil?

Ask a question.

How does the way water falls on soil change the amount of soil moved?

State a hypothesis.

You will conduct 2 experiments. You will make and test 2 hypotheses. Why do you think scientists sometimes conduct 2 experiments together?

____

____

If more water falls on soil, then will more, less, or about the same amount of soil be eroded? Write your **hypothesis.**

____

If water falls on soil faster, then will more, less, or about the same amount of soil be eroded? Write your **hypothesis.**

____

Identify and control variables.

In these **experiments,** water is the **variable** you will change. In one test you use more water. In a second test you let the water fall faster. You compare both to the control.

Test your hypothesis.

❶–❺ Follow the steps to perform your experiment. Record your data.

Collect and record your data.

Container	Water Added (mL)	Amount of Erosion Observed (Estimate the fraction of the soil that moved.)
Container A		
Container B		
Container C		

Interpret your data.

Analyze your data. Make circle graphs on a separate sheet of paper to show your data. Compare your data with the data from other groups.

State your conclusion.

Think about your first hypothesis. What conclusion can you draw from your chart? Does it agree with your **hypothesis? Communicate** your conclusion. Repeat for your second hypothesis.

____

____

____

____

Go Further

You observed how soil was eroded. Would your results change if you tested sand, mud, or rocks instead? How would changing the slope of the soil affect your results? Design and carry out a plan to investigate these or other questions you may have.

____

Self-Assessment Checklist	
I stated my **hypotheses** about how the way water falls on soil affects erosion.	____
I followed instructions to test my **hypotheses** and **observed** the results.	____
I **collected data** in a chart and **estimated** how much soil was eroded.	____
I compared the data with the data from other groups.	____
I **communicated** my conclusions.	____

Notes for Home: Your child did an activity to examine factors that affect how erosion shapes land.

Home Activity: With your child, discuss how erosion in the past has had an effect on your area or on an area you've visited.

Name ____________________________________ **Lab zone Directed Inquiry**

Use with Chapter 11, page 316

Explore: What properties cause liquids to form layers?

Explain Your Results

1. **Infer** Which liquid has the highest density? Which has the lowest density? How do you know?

____

____

____

2. Which object has the highest density? Which has the lowest density? How do you know?

____

____

____

Self-Assessment Checklist	
I followed instructions to pour liquids into a cup in the correct order.	______
I **observed** that the liquids form layers.	______
I followed instructions to drop objects into the cup.	______
I **made inferences** about which liquids had the highest and lowest density.	______
I **made inferences** about which objects had the highest and lowest density and gave reasons for my inferences.	______

Notes for Home: Your child did an activity to find out why liquids of different densities form layers.
Home Activity: With your child, discuss why a jar of cotton balls is lighter than a jar of paper clips.

Name ______________________

Use with Chapter 11, pp. 338–339

Investigate: How can you change the properties of glue?

❷–❻ Record the data you collect about the properties of glue and of the new substance.

Property	Observations	
	Glue	New Substance
Color		
Texture		
State of Matter (solid, liquid, gas)		
Odor		

Explain Your Results

1. How are the physical properties of the new substance and the glue alike?

____

What differences did you **observe?**

____

____

____

____

____

2. Would the new substance be a good glue? Explain.

____

Name ______________________________

Go Further

If you used a different amount of borax solution, would the substance have the same properties? Develop a plan for a safe, simple investigation to answer this question or one of your own. With teacher permission, carry out the plan you designed.

____

____

____

____

Self-Assessment Checklist	
I followed instructions to add water to the glue and **observed** the properties of the mixture of glue and water.	____
I followed instructions to add borax solution to the glue and water, stirred, **observed** what happened, and investigated the properties of the new substance.	____
I recorded **data** about the properties of glue and of the new substance.	____
I **observed** the similarities and differences between the new substance and the glue.	____
I made an **inference** about whether or not the new substance would be a good glue.	____

Notes for Home: Your child combined glue and a solution of borax and water to make a new substance and observed its properties.
Home Activity: With your child, experiment with modeling clay. Compare the properties of modeling clay to the properties of the substance created in class.

Lab zone **Activity**

Is it a chemical or physical change?

Materials

What to Do

1. Use the masking tape and a pencil to make a label for each cup. Label one cup Sugar. Label the other cup Baking Soda.
2. Put one spoonful of sugar in the cup labeled Sugar.
3. Add 4 spoonfuls of vinegar to the cup. Stir the vinegar and sugar with the spoon for one minute. **Observe** and record what happens.
4. Use a different spoon to put one spoonful of baking soda in the cup labeled Baking Soda.
5. Add 4 spoonfuls of vinegar to the cup. Observe and record what happens.

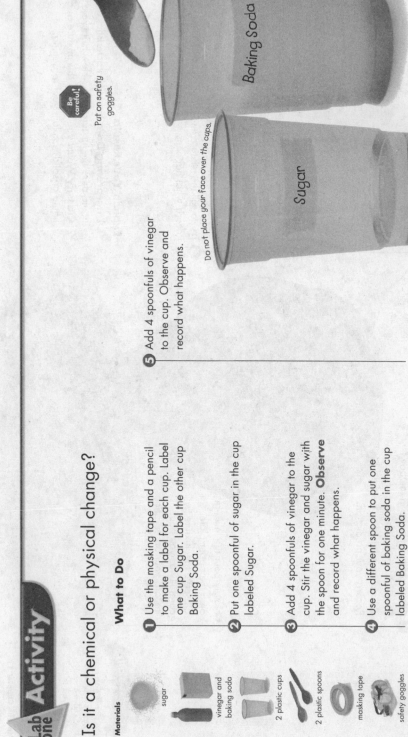

Be careful! Put on safety goggles.

Do not place your face over the cups.

Process Skills

You can **interpret data** about what happens in each cup to **infer** whether a physical or chemical change takes place.

Explain Your Results

1. **Infer** In which cup did a physical change take place? A chemical change?
2. **Interpreting Data** What evidence did you use to answer question 1?

Use with Chapter 11

21

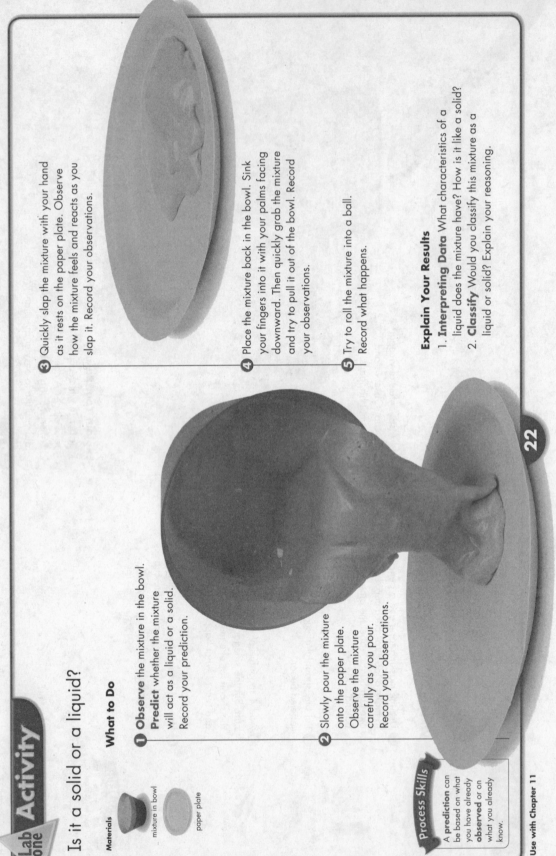

Lab zone **Activity**

Is it a solid or a liquid?

Materials

mixture in bowl

paper plate

What to Do

1. **Observe** the mixture in the bowl. **Predict** whether the mixture will act as a liquid or a solid. Record your prediction.

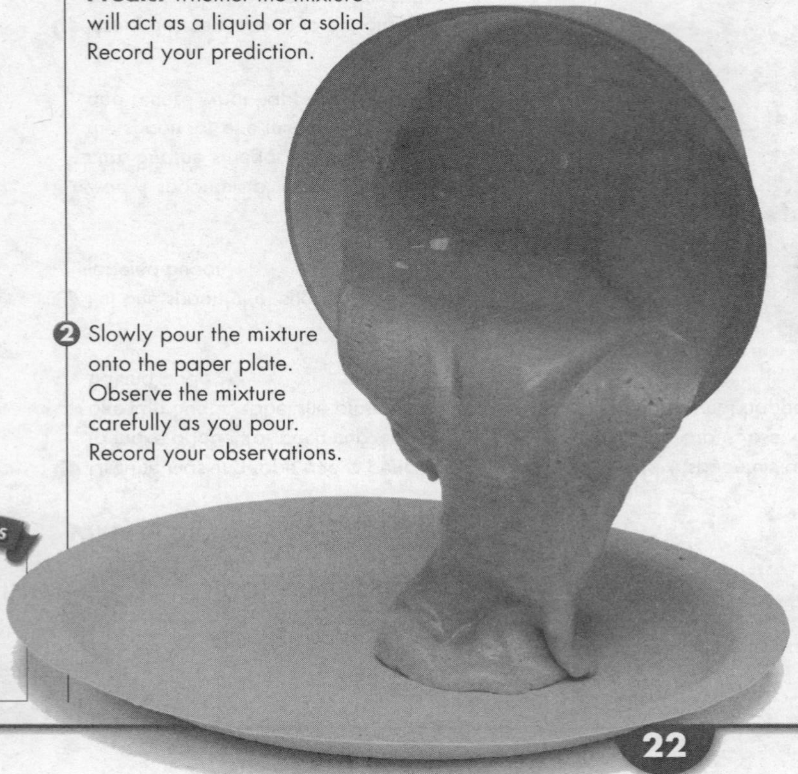

2. Slowly pour the mixture onto the paper plate. Observe the mixture carefully as you pour. Record your observations.

3. Quickly slap the mixture with your hand as it rests on the paper plate. Observe how the mixture feels and reacts as you slap it. Record your observations.

4. Place the mixture back in the bowl. Sink your fingers into it with your palms facing downward. Then quickly grab the mixture and try to pull it out of the bowl. Record your observations.

5. Try to roll the mixture into a ball. Record what happens.

Process Skills

A **prediction** can be based on what you have already **observed** or on what you already know.

Explain Your Results

1. **Interpreting Data** What characteristics of a liquid does the mixture have? How is it like a solid?
2. **Classify** Would you classify this mixture as a liquid or solid? Explain your reasoning.

Use with Chapter 11

22

Name ______________________________

Use with page 21

Is it a chemical or physical change?

3. Put on safety goggles. Add 4 spoonfuls of vinegar to the cup with sugar. Stir the vinegar and sugar with the spoon for one minute. **Observe** and record what happens.

5. Add 4 spoonfuls of vinegar to the cup with baking soda. Do not place your face over the cup. Observe and record what happens.

	Observations
Sugar	
Baking Soda	

Explain Your Results

1. **Infer:** In which cup did a physical change take place? A chemical change?

____

____

____

2. **Interpreting Data:** What evidence did you use to answer question 1?

____

____

Name ______________________

Use with page 21

Self-Assessment Checklist	
I followed instructions to label one cup *Sugar* and the other cup *Baking Soda.*	____
I followed instructions to put each substance in the correct cup.	____
I **observed** what happened when I added vinegar to sugar and to baking soda.	____
I made an **inference** about what kind of reaction took place in which cup.	____
I **interpreted my data** in order to explain my answer to question 1.	____

Notes for Home: Your child did an activity to **interpret data** in order to **infer** whether a physical or a chemical reaction took place.
Home Activity: With your child, find an example of a physical reaction and an example of a chemical reaction in your home or neighborhood.

Name ______________________________

Use with page 22

Is it a solid or a liquid?

❶ **Observe** the mixture in the bowl. **Predict** whether the mixture will act as a liquid or a solid. Record your prediction.

____

____

❷–❺ Slowly pour the mixture onto the paper plate. Observe the mixture carefully as you pour. Record your observations. Quickly slap the mixture with your hand as it rests on the paper plate. Observe how the mixture feels and reacts as you slap it. Record your observations. Place the mixture back in the bowl. Sink your fingers into it with your palms facing downward. Then quickly grab the mixture and try to pull it out of the bowl. Record your observations. Try to roll the mixture into a ball. Record your observations.

	Observations
Mixture in bowl	
Mixture poured onto paper plate	
Slapping the mixture	
Pulling the mixture	
Rolling the mixture into a ball	

Name ______________________________

Use with page 22

Explain Your Results

1. Interpreting Data: What characteristics of a liquid does the mixture have? How is it like a solid?

____

____

____

2. Classify: Would you classify this mixture as a liquid or solid? Explain your reasoning.

____

____

____

Self-Assessment Checklist	
I **observed** the mixture in the bowl.	___
I **predicted** whether the mixture would act as a liquid or as a solid.	___
I **observed** the mixture in different situations and recorded my observations.	___
I **interpreted my data** to describe how the mixture is like a liquid and how it is like a solid.	___
I explained whether I would **classify** the mixture as a liquid or as a solid.	___

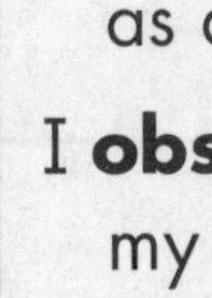

Notes for Home: Your child did an activity to **observe** a mixture and determine from its properties whether it is a liquid or a solid.
Home Activity: With your child, discuss how you could tell if a substance was a gas.

Explore: How can you make things warmer?

1. Touch a paper clip. **Observe**. Does it feel warm?

 ____

2. Bend one end back and forth 4 times quickly. Quickly touch the bent part. **Observe**.

 ____

3. Touch an eraser. Rub it on paper for 1 minute. Quickly touch the part you rubbed on the paper. **Observe**.

 ____

4. Rub your hands together for 15 seconds. **Observe**.

 ____

Explain Your Results

1. How did bending change the paper clip?

 ____

2. What happened when the eraser rubbed against the paper? What happened when you rubbed one hand against the other?

 ____

3. What can you **infer** about what happens when one object rubs against another?

 ____

Self-Assessment Checklist	
I touched a paper clip and **observed** whether it felt warm.	____
I bent a paper clip back and forth, **observed** whether or not it felt warm, and reported how bending changed the paper clip.	____
I rubbed an eraser on paper for 1 minute, **observed** the part I rubbed, and described what happened.	____
I rubbed my hands together, **observed** how they felt, and described what happened.	____
I made an **inference** about what happens when one object rubs against another.	____

Notes for Home: Your child did an activity to **observe** that when one object rubs against another, it feels warmer.
Home Activity: With your child, **predict** whether more heat is produced if you rub your hands together quickly or if you rub them slowly.

Name ______________________________

Use with Chapter 12, pp. 360–361

Investigate: How are thermal energy and temperature different?

❷–❺ Record the temperature of the water in each cup on your chart. After a cup's ice cube melts, record the water temperature in that cup, and add another ice cube to that cup. When the temperature in a cup reaches 10°C stop adding ice cubes to the cup.

	Temperature of Water (°C)	
	Cup A (300 mL water)	**Cup B** (150 mL water)
Before adding ice		
After 1 ice cube melts		
After 2 ice cubes melt		
After 3 ice cubes melt		
After 4 ice cubes melt		
After 5 ice cubes melt		
After 6 ice cubes melt		
After 7 ice cubes melt		
After 8 ice cubes melt		
After 9 ice cubes melt		
After 10 ice cubes melt		
After 11 ice cubes melt		
After 12 ice cubes melt		
After 13 ice cubes melt		

Number of ice cubes completely melted when temperature reached 10°C:		

Make a bar graph to show your data.

Thermal Energy

Number of Ice Cubes		
13		
12		
11		
10		
9		
8		
7		
6		
5		
4		
3		
2		
1		
0		
	Cup A (300 mL water)	**Cup B** (150 mL water)

Name ______________________________

Use with Chapter 12, pp. 360–361

Explain Your Results

1. Which cup has more thermal energy? How do you know?

____

____

2. Suppose you used 600 mL of your warm water. **Predict** how many ice cubes would be needed to lower the temperature to 10°C. How could you test your prediction?

____

____

____

Go Further

Develop and conduct a scientific investigation to test the prediction you made. Design any tables, charts, graphs, or diagrams to help record, display, and interpret your data.

Self-Assessment Checklist	
I followed instructions to prepare the cups and recorded the temperature of the water in each cup.	____
I followed directions to add ice cubes and to **observe** and record temperature data in a chart.	____
I constructed a graph to organize my data.	____
I determined which cup had more thermal energy.	____
I **predicted** how much ice would lower the temperature of 600 mL of warm water to 10°C.	____

Notes for Home: Your child did an activity to observe the difference between temperature and heat.
Home Activity: With your child, discuss whether it would take more energy to raise the temperature of a large house or a small house.

Lab zone **Activity**

Which material is the best heat conductor?

Materials

What to Do

1. Use a small ball of margarine to stick a bead onto the handle of each spoon. The beads should all be at the same height on the spoons.

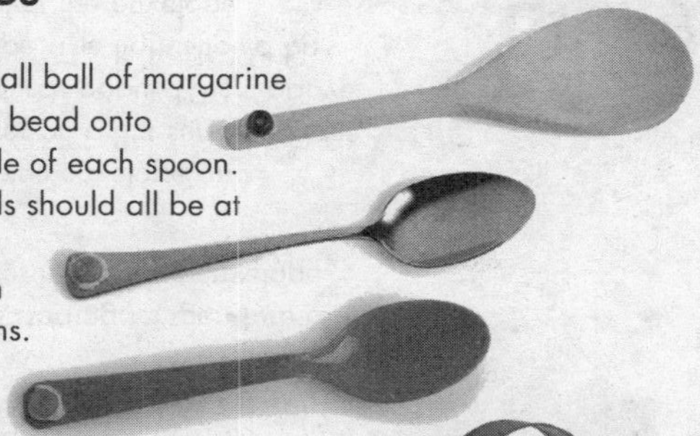

2. Fill the cup half full of very warm water.

3. Place the spoons into the cup of very warm water.

4. **Observe** the margarine and the beads for several minutes. Record what happens.

Be careful! Use care when working with very warm water. Clean up spills right away.

Explain Your Results

1. What happened to the margarine and the beads?
2. What caused this to happen?
3. **Infer** Which material is the best conductor: metal, wood, or plastic? Use the results of this activity to support your answer.

Process Skills

When you make an **inference,** be sure you can support it with facts and **observations.**

Use with Chapter 12

23

Lab zone **Activity**

Do all materials absorb the same amount of thermal energy?

Materials

construction paper

stapler

3 thermometers

light source

clock

Process Skills

When you **collect data,** you gather information about observations and measurements.

What to Do

1. Fold the bottom of each sheet of construction paper so that it is within 5 cm of the top edge. Staple the side edges to form an envelope for a thermometer.
2. Place a thermometer in each of the envelopes.
3. Record the starting temperature of the thermometer in the blue envelope.
4. Place the blue envelope and thermometer on a flat surface. Place the light source about 10 cm above the envelope. The light should be centered over the envelope.

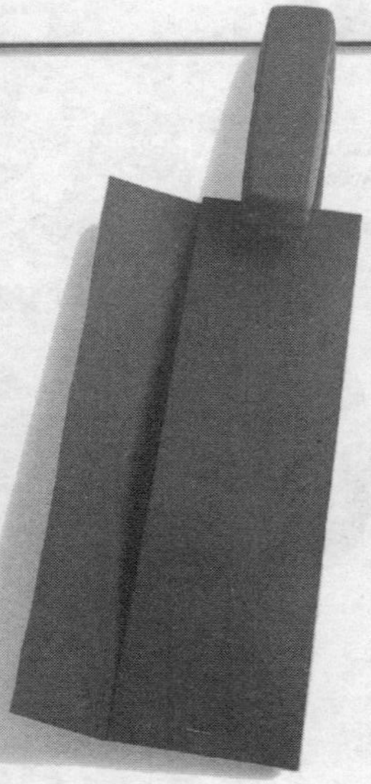

5. **Measure** and record the temperature every minute for 10 minutes.
6. Repeat steps 3–5 with the other two envelopes.

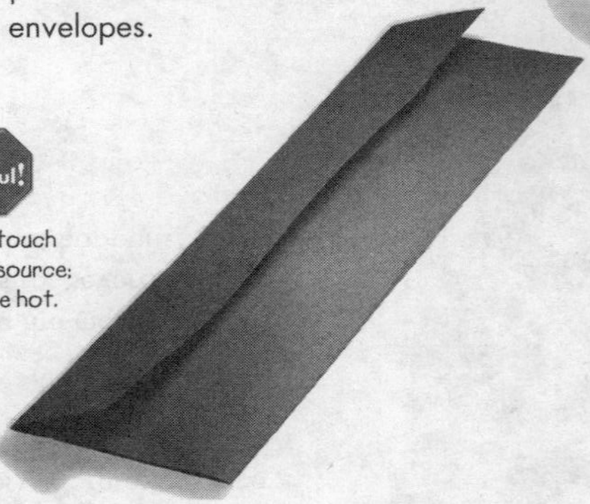

Be careful! Do not touch the light source; it may be hot.

Explain Your Results

1. Why didn't you put all three envelopes under the light at the same time? Hint: Think about controlling variables.
2. Graph your **data.** Use different colored pens or pencils to represent the different colors of construction paper. Include a key to show which line represents each color of paper.
3. **Infer** Which material absorbed the most thermal energy? How do you know?

Use with Chapter 12

24

Name ______________________________

Use with page 23

Which material is the best heat conductor?

Explain Your Results

1. What happened to the margarine and the beads?

____

____

____

2. What caused this to happen?

____

____

3. Infer: Which material is the best conductor of heat: metal, wood, or plastic? Use the results of this activity to support your answer.

____

____

____

____

Name ______________________

Self-Assessment Checklist	
I followed instructions to use margarine to stick a bead onto the handle of each spoon.	_____
I followed instructions to fill the cups with warm water and place the spoons in the cups.	_____
I **observed** the margarine and the beads for several minutes and recorded what happened.	_____
I explained what caused the **observed** results.	_____
I made an **inference** about which material is the best conductor of heat and supported my answer.	_____

Notes for Home: Your child did an activity to **observe** which material makes the best heat conductor.
Home Activity: With your child, find an object in your home that is designed to keep in heat and **observe** the materials from which it is made.

Name ______________________________

Use with page 24

Do all materials absorb the same amount of thermal energy?

3 Record the starting temperature of the thermometer in the blue envelope.

Time	Temperature (°C)		
	Blue Envelope	**White Envelope**	**Black Envelope**
Start			
1 minute			
2 minutes			
3 minutes			
4 minutes			
5 minutes			
6 minutes			
7 minutes			
8 minutes			
9 minutes			
10 minutes			

5–6 **Measure** and record the temperature every minute for 10 minutes. Repeat steps 3–5 with the other two envelopes.

Explain Your Results

1. Why didn't you put all three envelopes under the light at the same time? Hint: Think about controlling variables.

____

____

____

Name ______________________________

Use with page 24

2. Graph your **data.** Use different colored pens or pencils to represent the different colors of construction paper. Include a key to show which line represents each color of paper.

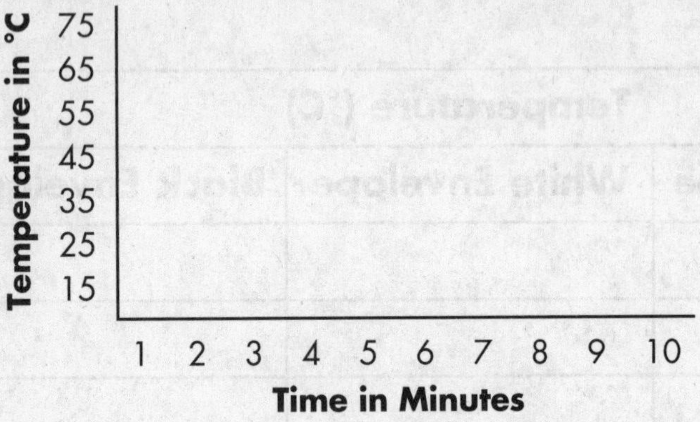

3. Infer: Which material absorbed the most amount of thermal energy? How do you know?

____

____

____

Self-Assessment Checklist	
I followed instructions to make three envelopes and put them under the light.	______
I **measured** and recorded the temperature of each envelope every minute for 10 minutes.	______
I explained why I didn't put all three envelopes under the light at the same time.	______
I graphed my **data** using different colors and included a key.	______
I made an **inference** about the material that absorbed the most amount of thermal energy.	______

Notes for Home: Your child did an activity to **collect data** about how much thermal energy different materials absorb.
Home Activity: With your child, discuss which colors would be the best to wear on a cold day.

Name ______________________________

Use with Chapter 13, p. 372

Explore: How can static electricity affect objects?

Explain Your Results

1. What happened as you brought together your balloon and your cloth? your balloon and the balloon of another group?

____

____

2. Infer: How do objects with opposite charges affect each other? How do objects with the same charge affect each other?

____

____

Self-Assessment Checklist	
I followed instructions to rub the balloon with a wool cloth for about 1 minute.	______
I **observed** what happened when the balloon and the cloth were brought closer together.	______
I **observed** what happened when the balloon was brought near the balloon of another group.	______
I described what happened in each of the **observed** situations.	______
I made an **inference** about how charged objects affect each other.	______

Notes for Home: Your child did an activity to explore how electrically charged objects affect each other.
Home Activity: With your child, discuss why the balloons and the cloth studied in class had an electric charge.

Name ______________________________

Use with Chapter 13, pp. 394–395

Investigate: What is an electromagnet?

2. Hold a paper clip near the head of a bolt. Record your **observations.**
3. Put a battery in the battery holder. Attach both ends of the wire to it. Find how many paper clips your electromagnet can pick up. Record your result in the chart.
4. Wrap 20 more coils of wire around the bolt. **Predict** how many clips your electromagnet can pick up now.

____

____

Find out. Record your result.

Number of Coils	Number of Paper Clips Picked Up
30 coils (no battery)	
30 coils	
50 coils	

5. Make a bar graph of your results, or select a different way to show your results.

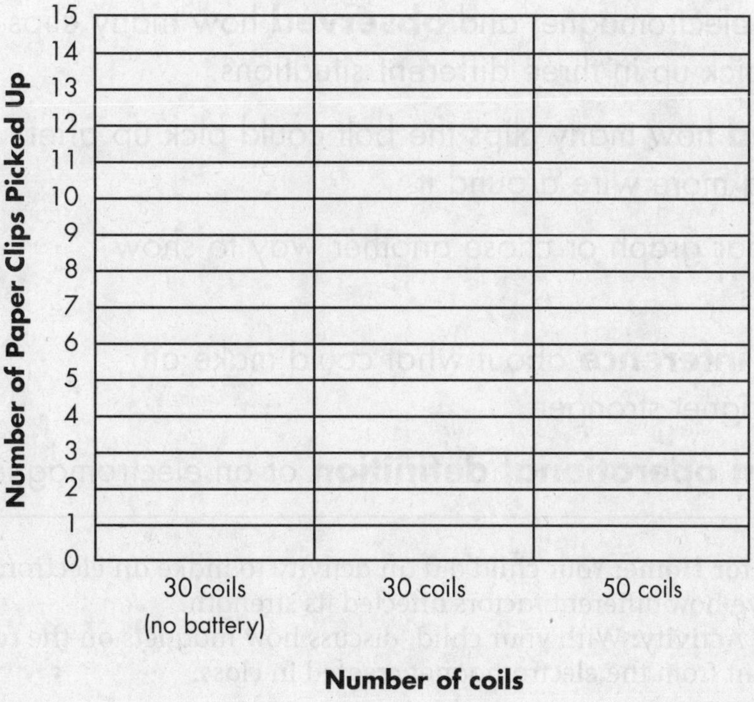

Explain Your Results

1. Infer: What can make an electromagnet stronger?

____

2. Make an **operational definition** of an electromagnet.

____

____

____

____

Go Further

Which objects will a magnet attract? Use your electromagnet as a tool. Develop and carry out a plan to answer this or another question you may have. Write instructions others could use to repeat your investigation.

____

____

____

Self-Assessment Checklist	
I made an electromagnet and **observed** how many clips it could pick up in three different situations.	_____
I **predicted** how many clips the bolt could pick up after wrapping more wire around it.	_____
I made a bar graph or chose another way to show my results.	_____
I made an **inference** about what could make an electromagnet stronger.	_____
I **made an operational definition** of an electromagnet.	_____

Notes for Home: Your child did an activity to make an electromagnet and **observe** how different factors affected its strength.
Home Activity: With your child, discuss how magnets on the refrigerator are different from the electromagnet created in class.

Lab zone **Activity**

How can you make a charge detector?

Materials

Process Skills

When you **communicate** activity results, be sure to state all the necessary information clearly.

What to Do

1. Put on your safety goggles. Stick the nail about halfway through the hole in the round piece of cardboard.

2. Tie the piece of thread around the nail near the sharp end. The ends of the thread should be even after it has been tied on the nail.

Be careful! Use care when handling the nail.

3. Cut two small pieces of foil. Each piece should be about 1 cm x 2 cm. Tape one piece to each end of the thread. Be sure the pieces of tape are very small.

4. Place the cardboard on top of the cup with the thread pieces hanging down. Tape the cardboard to the cup.

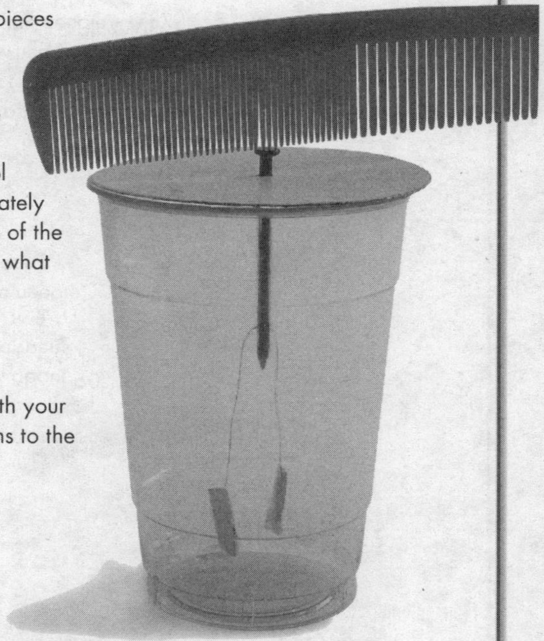

5. Rub the comb with the wool cloth several times. Immediately touch the comb to the head of the nail. **Observe** and record what happens to the foil pieces.

6. Touch the top of the nail with your finger. Record what happens to the foil strips.

Explain Your Results

1. What happened to the foil pieces when the comb touched the nail head?
2. What happened when you touched the nail head with your finger?
3. **Communicate** Write a paragraph that explains what caused the results in this activity.
   Hint: Rubbing the comb with the cloth causes the comb to get an electric charge.

Lab zone **Activity**

How can you make a compass?

Materials

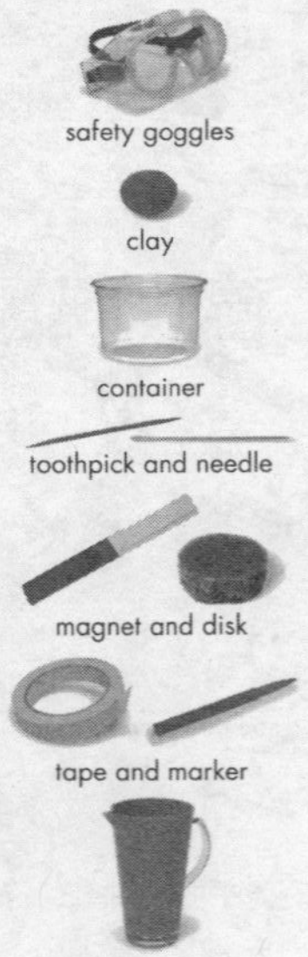

Process Skills

When you make a **prediction,** be sure to consider all the facts and observations you have gathered.

What to Do

1. Put on your safety goggles. Place a piece of modeling clay in the center of the plastic container. Stick one end of the toothpick into the modeling clay so that the toothpick stands upright.

2. To magnetize the needle, rub one end of the magnet over the needle about 30 times. Rub in the same direction with the same end of the magnet each time. When you are finished with the magnet, place it at least a meter away from the needle.

Be careful with the needle.

3. Tape the needle to the disk. Use a small piece of tape.

4. Place the disk in the plastic container, sticking it into the toothpick. The needle should be facing up.

5. Pour water into the container until the disk just floats. As the disk floats, it will turn and one end of the needle will point north. Use a marker to mark this end on your "compass."

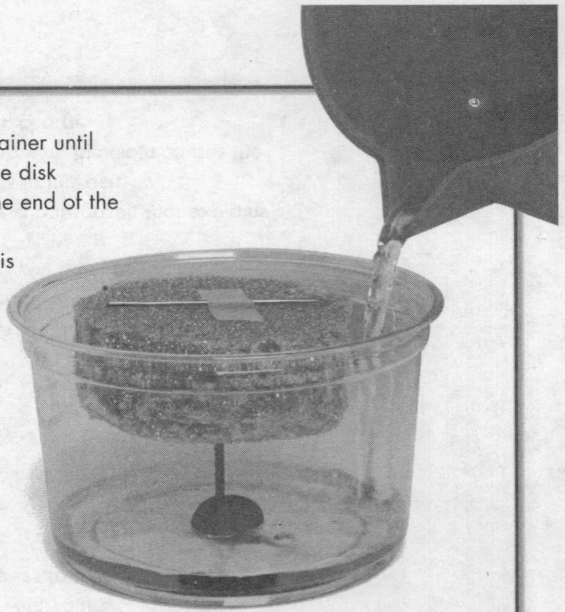

6. Carefully turn the container about 90° to the right. Record what happens.

7. Hold the magnet next to the needle and then move it away. Record what happens.

Explain Your Results

1. **Infer** What happened to the needle when you turned the container? Why?
2. **Infer** What happened when you placed the magnet near the needle? Why?
3. **Predict** In what direction would your compass point if you moved it to another part of the room? Why?

Use with Chapter 13

26

Name ________________________________

Use with page 25

How can you make a charge detector?

Explain Your Results

1. What happened to the foil pieces when the comb touched the nail head?

____

2. What happened when you touched the nail head with your finger?

____

3. **Communicate:** Write a paragraph that explains what caused the results in this activity. Hint: Rubbing the comb with the cloth causes the comb to get an electric charge.

____

____

____

Self-Assessment Checklist	
I followed instructions to set up the nail and foil and place the cardboard on the cup.	____
I followed instructions to rub the comb with the wool cloth several times.	____
I touched the comb to the head of the nail and **observed** and recorded what happened.	____
I touched the top of the nail with a finger and explained what happened.	____
I **communicated** what caused the results in this activity in a paragraph.	____

Notes for Home: Your child did an activity to make a charge detector.
Home Activity: With your child, rub a balloon with a piece of cloth and **observe** what happens.

Name ____________________________________

Use with page 26

How can you make a compass?

Explain Your Results

1. Infer: What happened to the needle when you turned the container? Why?

____

____

2. Infer: What happened when you placed the magnet near the needle? Why?

____

____

____

3. Predict: In what direction would your compass point if you moved it to another part of the room? Why?

____

____

Self-Assessment Checklist	
I followed instructions to magnetize the needle and tape it to the disk.	______
I followed instructions to set up the disk inside the container.	______
I made an **inference** about what happened when I turned the container.	______
I made an **inference** about what happened when I placed the magnet near the needle.	______
I **predicted** where my compass would point if I moved it to another part of the room.	______

Notes for Home: Your child did an activity to make a compass.
Home Activity: With your child, discuss what attracts the compass needle to Earth's magnetic north.

Explore: What makes sound change?

Explain Your Results

1. How did adding more water affect the pitch?

____

____

2. Describe how plucking harder changes the volume.

____

____

3. Infer: How does the length of the string affect the pitch?

____

____

Self-Assessment Checklist	
I followed instructions to tie a string around a bottle and filled it $\frac{1}{3}$ full with water.	______
I plucked the string and **observed** the sound.	______
I filled the bottle with water and described the change in pitch.	______
I plucked the string gently and hard and described how plucking harder changed the volume.	______
I shortened how far the bottle hung and made an **inference** about how that affected the pitch.	______

Notes for Home: Your child did an activity to explore different factors that cause changes in sound.
Home Activity: With your child, tap glasses filled with different amounts of water with a spoon and describe how the sound changes.

Name ______________________

Guided Inquiry

Use with Chapter 14, pp. 426–427

Investigate: How is light reflected and refracted?

❷ Hold the flashlight about 60 cm back from the box. Shine the light through the slits. **Observe** the light's path inside the box. Which objects are opaque? Do you see 2 straight lines?

____

❸–❹ Tilt a mirror in the box to reflect the light. **Observe** the light's path. Put an empty plastic cup in the box. Add water. Observe how light passes through the cup and how it is refracted. What things are transparent?

____

❺ Draw a sketch or diagram to show the path of the light from the flashlight, through the slits, through the water, and beyond.

Explain Your Results

1. Compare how light is affected by the air, the cup, the water, the box, the black paper, and the mirror. Use the terms *reflect, refract, absorb, opaque,* and *transparent.*

____

____

____

____

____

2. Describe the light's path through the box and the cup with water. **Infer** what happens when light travels from air to water.

____

____

____

____

Go Further

How is light affected by translucent materials, such as wax paper? Develop and carry out a written plan to answer this question or one of your own. When finished, give an oral report to your class or make a written report in your science journal.

____

____

Self-Assessment Checklist	
I followed instructions to prepare the box.	____
I **observed** how light was affected by the air, cup, water, box, black paper, and mirror.	____
I described and drew a sketch or a diagram of the path of the light from the flashlight.	____
I compared how the light was affected by the air, cup, water, box, black paper, and mirror using the terms *reflect, refract, absorb, opaque* and *transparent.*	____
I made an **inference** about what happens when light travels from air to water.	____

Notes for Home: Your child did an activity to **observe** that light travels in straight lines and to **observe** how it is reflected, refracted, and absorbed.
Home Activity: With your child, **observe** a light source such as a streetlight or a sunny window and note how the light moves.

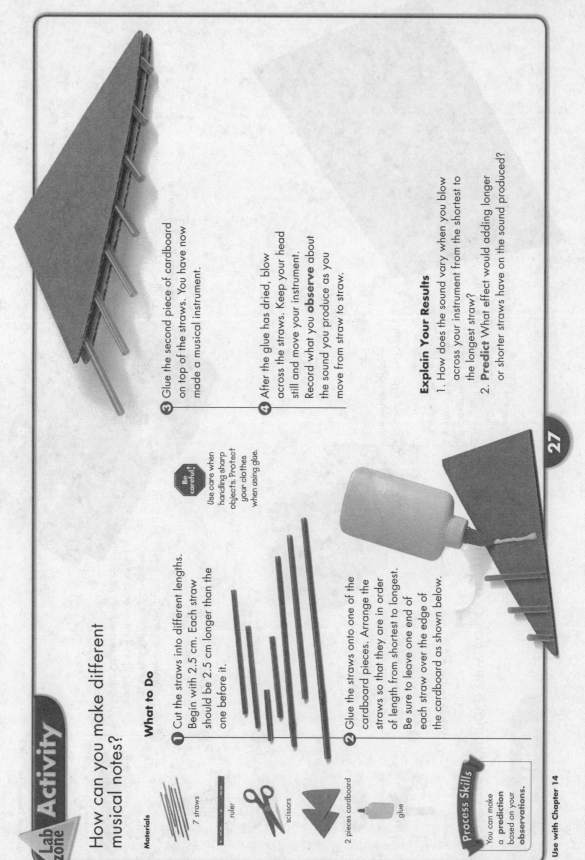

Lab zone **Activity**

How can you make different musical notes?

Materials

What to Do

1. Cut the straws into different lengths. Begin with 2.5 cm. Each straw should be 2.5 cm longer than the one before it.

Be careful! Use care when handling sharp objects. Protect your clothes when using glue.

2. Glue the straws onto one of the cardboard pieces. Arrange the straws so that they are in order of length from shortest to longest. Be sure to leave one end of each straw over the edge of the cardboard as shown below.

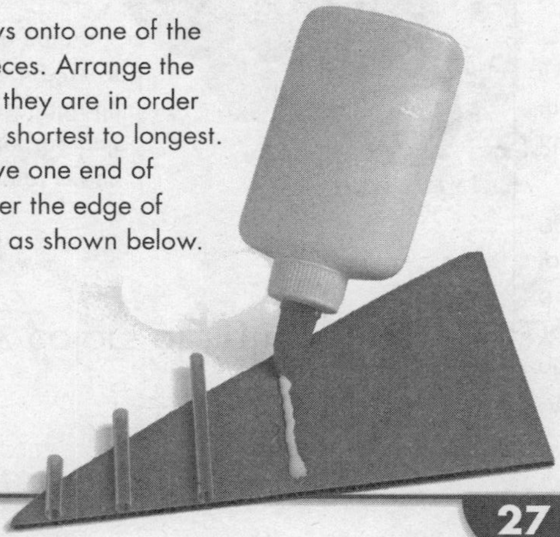

3. Glue the second piece of cardboard on top of the straws. You have now made a musical instrument.

4. After the glue has dried, blow across the straws. Keep your head still and move your instrument. Record what you **observe** about the sound you produce as you move from straw to straw.

Explain Your Results

1. How does the sound vary when you blow across your instrument from the shortest to the longest straw?
2. **Predict** What effect would adding longer or shorter straws have on the sound produced?

Process Skills

You can make a **prediction** based on your **observations.**

Lab zone **Activity**

How can you make new colors of light?

Materials

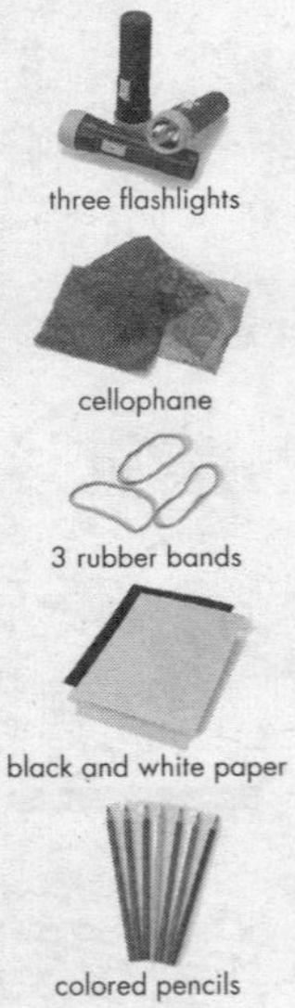

What to Do

1. Place the piece of green cellophane over the bulb end of one flashlight. Pull the cellophane tightly and hold it in place with a rubber band.

2. Repeat step 1 with the red and blue cellophane.
3. Hold the black paper upright near the end of a table.
4. Lay the flashlights on the table. Line them up so that they are pointing at the black paper. Turn on each of the flashlights. **Observe** the light on the black paper.

5. Move the flashlights so that circles of light on the paper overlap. Your light pattern should look like a clover leaf. Use colored pencils to draw the pattern of light that appears on the black paper.
6. Repeat steps 3–5 with the white paper.

Process Skills

You can **infer** the colors of white light by mixing colors made by flashlights.

Explain Your Results

1. Red, blue, and green are the primary colors of light. How do they differ from the primary colors of paint?
2. What color is produced when the three colors of light are mixed? Hint: Look at the center of the clover leaf.
3. **Infer** How does this activity show that white light is made of different colors?

Use with Chapter 14

28

Name ______________________

Use with page 27

How can you make different musical notes?

Explain Your Results

1. How does the sound vary when you blow across your instrument from the shortest to the longest straw?

____

____

2. **Predict:** What effect would adding longer straws have on the sound produced?

____

Self-Assessment Checklist	
I followed instructions to cut the straws into different lengths.	______
I followed instructions to glue together the straws and cardboard to make a musical instrument.	______
I **observed** the sound produced by blowing into the different straws.	______
I described how the sound varied from the shortest to the longest straw.	______
I **predicted** what effect adding longer straws would have on the sound produced.	______

Notes for Home: Your child did an activity to **observe** how to make different musical notes.
Home Activity: With your child, **observe** a picture of a musical instrument and discuss which of its features would affect the pitch of sound.

Name ______________________

Use with page 28

How can you make new colors of light?

❹ Lay the flashlights on the table. Line them up so that they are pointing at the black paper. Turn on each of the flashlights. **Observe** the light on the black paper.

____

Explain Your Results

1. What color is produced when the three colors of light are mixed? Hint: Look at the center of the clover leaf.

____

2. Infer: How does this activity show that white light is made of different colors?

____

____

Self-Assessment Checklist	
I followed instructions to put cellophane on the flashlights and hold the black paper upright.	____
I pointed the flashlights at the black paper, turned them on, and **observed** the light.	____
I used colored pencils and white paper to draw the pattern of light.	____
I named the color that was produced when the three colors of light were mixed.	____
I **inferred** about how this activity shows that white light is made of different colors.	____

Notes for Home: Your child did an activity to examine how to make new colors of light.
Home Activity: With your child, discuss how light causes objects to be different colors.

Name ____________________

Lab zone **Directed Inquiry**

Use with Chapter 15, p. 436

Explore: What can change a marble's speed?

❶ Roll a marble down a ramp. Time how long it takes to move 180 cm. Find the speed.

____

❷ **Predict** how raising the ramp would change the speed.

____

____

Explain Your Results

1. Interpret Data: Make a bar graph to show your results.

Speed of Marble on Ramp at Different Heights

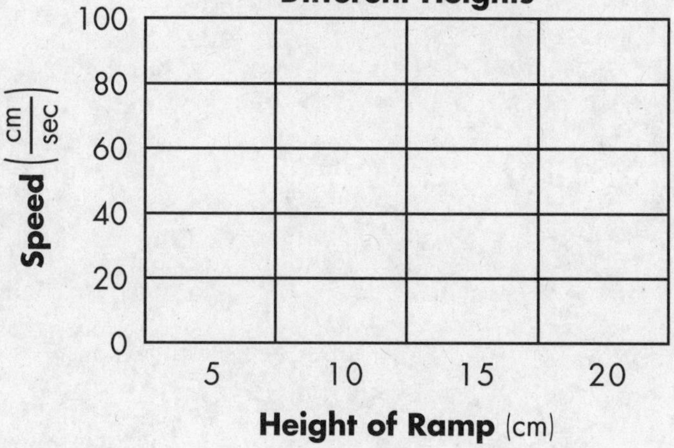

2. Infer: How did raising the ramp change the speed of the marble?

____

Name ______________________________

Self-Assessment Checklist	
I followed instructions to roll a marble down the ramp and time how long it took to move 180 cm.	______
I found the speed of my marble.	______
I **predicted** how raising the ramp would change the speed and tested my **prediction**.	______
I **interpreted my data** by making a bar graph of my results.	______
I made an **inference** about how raising the ramp changed the speed of the marble.	______

Notes for Home: Your child did an activity to explore how raising the height of a ramp changes the speed of a marble.
Home Activity: With your child, think of two other ways the speed of the marble could be increased.

Name ______________________________

Use with Chapter 15, pp. 450–451

Investigate: How does friction affect motion?

❸ When each object reaches the bottom of the ramp, record the angle. Repeat 2 more times. **Collect** and record your **data** in the chart.

❹ Based on your **observations, predict** what would happen if you replaced the sandpaper with waxed paper.

____

____

Test your **prediction** 3 times. Record your **data.** Find the averages.

	Angle at Which Object Reached Bottom of Ramp			
Surface	**Sandpaper**		**Waxed Paper**	
Object	**Car**	**Eraser**	**Car**	**Eraser**
Trial 1				
Trial 2				
Trial 3				
Average				

❺ Make a bar graph of your results.

Average Angle at which Object Reached Bottom of Ramp

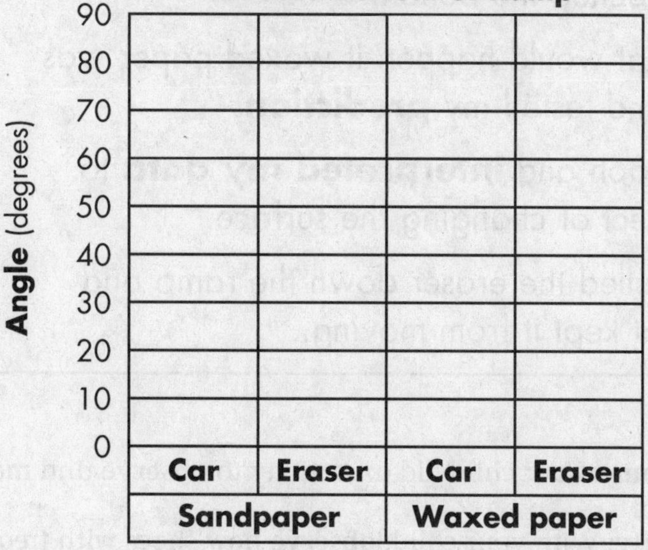

Explain Your Results

1. Interpreting Data: How did using waxed paper instead of sandpaper affect the angle at which the objects moved?

____

____

2. What force pulled the eraser down the ramp? What force kept the eraser from moving until the ramp was steep enough?

____

Go Further

How could you increase or decrease the force of friction between the objects and the ramp? Design and conduct a scientific investigation to find out. Provide evidence for your conclusion.

____

____

Self-Assessment Checklist	
I followed instructions to raise the ramp and **observed** its angle.	____
I **collected** and recorded **data** about the angle at which each object reached the bottom.	____
I **predicted** what would happen if waxed paper was used instead and tested my **prediction.**	____
I made a bar graph and **interpreted my data** to explain the effect of changing the surface.	____
I named what pulled the eraser down the ramp and described what kept it from moving.	____

Notes for Home: Your child did an activity to **observe** and measure the effects of friction.
Home Activity: With your child, **observe** how shoes with treads in the sole prevent slipping on a smooth surface.

Lab zone **Activity**

How can you tell if you are accelerating?

Materials

What to Do

1. Tie one end of the thread around the metal end of the pushpin. Stick the pushpin into one end of the cork.

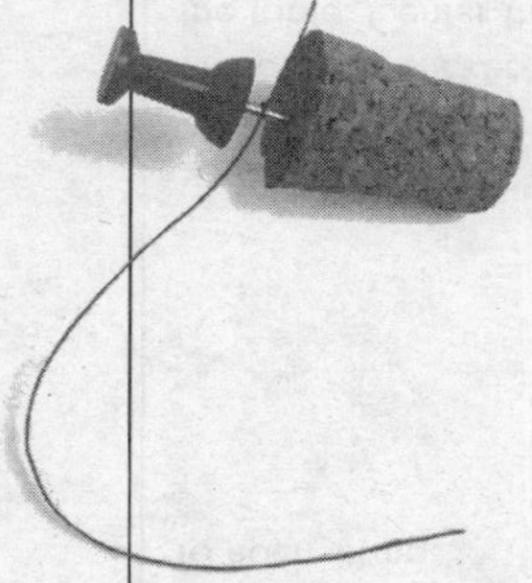

Be careful! Use care when handling sharp objects.

2. Glue the loose end of the thread to the inside of the bottle lid.

3. Fill the bottle about three-quarters full with water.
4. Put the cork into the bottle. Screw the lid tightly onto the bottle. The cork should float on top of the water.
5. Turn the bottle upside down and hold it in front of you. Suddenly begin to walk forward, keeping the bottle steady. Record what happens to the cork.
6. Repeat step 5 with each of the activities below.
   - Suddenly increase your walking speed.
   - Jump up in the air.
   - Turn in a circle.

Explain Your Results

1. **Interpret Data** In which of the activities did you accelerate? How do you know?
2. **Predict** What would happen to the cork if you were walking and stopped slowly? Test your prediction.

Process Skills

When you **interpret data,** make sure your statement is supported by the activity results.

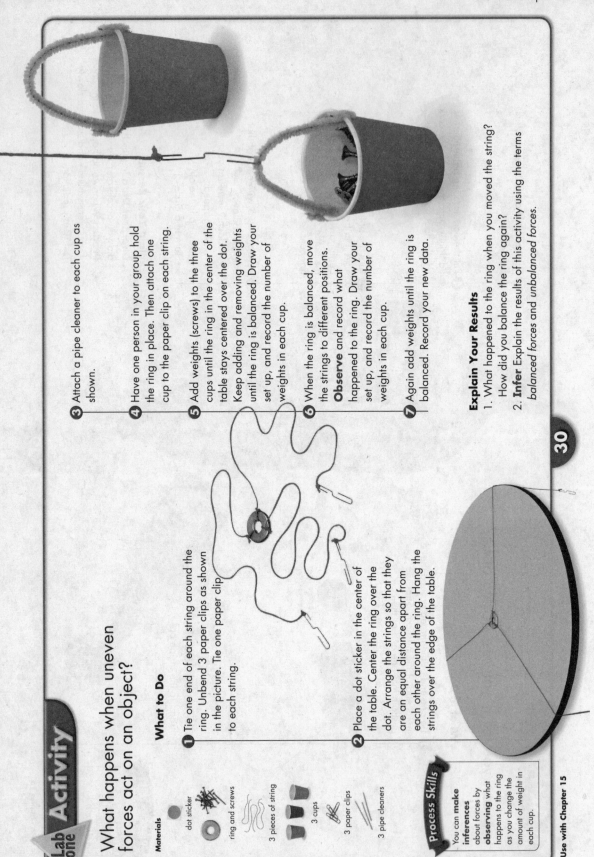

Lab zone **Activity**

What happens when uneven forces act on an object?

Materials

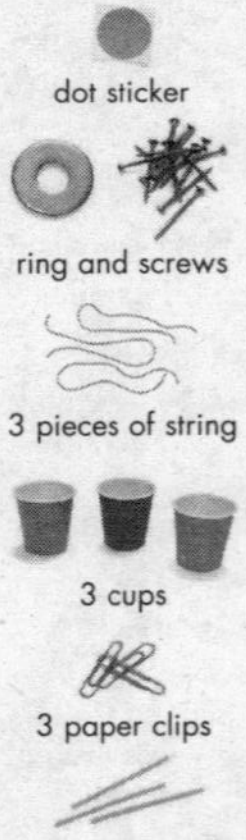

dot sticker

ring and screws

3 pieces of string

3 cups

3 paper clips

3 pipe cleaners

Process Skills

You can **make inferences** about forces by **observing** what happens to the ring as you change the amount of weight in each cup.

What to Do

1. Tie one end of each string around the ring. Unbend 3 paper clips as shown in the picture. Tie one paper clip to each string.

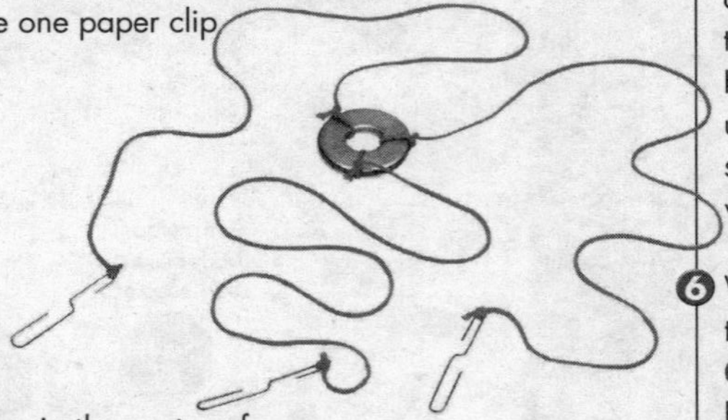

2. Place a dot sticker in the center of the table. Center the ring over the dot. Arrange the strings so that they are an equal distance apart from each other around the ring. Hang the strings over the edge of the table.

3. Attach a pipe cleaner to each cup as shown.
4. Have one person in your group hold the ring in place. Then attach one cup to the paper clip on each string.
5. Add weights (screws) to the three cups until the ring in the center of the table stays centered over the dot. Keep adding and removing weights until the ring is balanced. Draw your set up, and record the number of weights in each cup.
6. When the ring is balanced, move the strings to different positions. **Observe** and record what happened to the ring. Draw your set up, and record the number of weights in each cup.
7. Again add weights until the ring is balanced. Record your new data.

Explain Your Results

1. What happened to the ring when you moved the string? How did you balance the ring again?
2. **Infer** Explain the results of this activity using the terms *balanced forces* and *unbalanced forces*.

Use with Chapter 15

30

Name ______________________

Use with page 29

How can you tell if you are accelerating?

5–6 Turn the bottle upside down and hold it in front of you. Suddenly begin to walk forward, keeping the bottle steady. **Observe** and record what happens to the cork. Repeat step 5 with each of the following activities: suddenly increase your walking speed, jump in the air, turn in a circle.

Activity	Observation
Beginning to walk forward	
Increasing your walking speed	
Jumping in the air	
Turning in a circle	

Explain Your Results

1. **Interpret Data:** In which of the activities did you accelerate? How do you know?

____

____

____

____

2. **Predict:** What would happen to the cork if you were walking and stopped slowly? Test your prediction.

____

____

____

Name ______________________

Use with page 29

Self-Assessment Checklist	
I followed instructions to attach the cork to the lid and place it inside the bottle.	_____
I followed instructions to complete the different activities.	_____
I **observed** and recorded what happened to the cork in each situation.	_____
I **interpreted my data** to find the activities in which there was acceleration.	_____
I **predicted** what would happen if a person stopped walking slowly and tested my **prediction**.	_____

Notes for Home: Your child did an activity to investigate how to tell if you are accelerating.
Home Activity: With your child, **observe** signs that you are accelerating when riding in a moving vehicle.

Name ______________________

Use with page 30

What happens when uneven forces act on an object?

❺ Add weights to the three cups until the ring in the center of the table stays centered over the dot. Keep adding and removing weights until the ring is balanced. Draw your setup and record the number of rings in each cup.

Ring Location	Number of Weights in Each Cup		
	Cup A	Cup B	Cup C
over the dot			
over the dot			

❻ When the ring is balanced, move the strings to different positions. **Observe** and record what happened to the ring.

____

Draw your setup and record the number of weights in each cup.

Name ______________________________

Use with page 30

7. Again add weights until the ring is balanced. Record your new data.

Explain Your Results

1. What happened to the ring when you moved the string? How did you balance the ring again?

____

____

2. Infer: Explain the results of this activity using the terms *balanced forces* and *unbalanced forces.*

____

____

____

Self-Assessment Checklist	
I added weights until the ring was centered and drew my setup.	____
I moved the strings, **observed** what happened to the ring, and drew my setup.	____
I again added weights until the ring was balanced and recorded my new data.	____
I explained what happened when I moved the string and how I balanced the ring again.	____
I made an **inference** about how balanced forces and unbalanced forces related to this activity.	____

Notes for Home: Your child did an activity to **observe** what happens when uneven forces act on an object.
Home Activity: With your child, find and **observe** an example of uneven forces acting on an object in your home.

Name ______________________________ Lab zone **Directed Inquiry**

Use with Chapter 16, p. 460

Explore: How can a machine ring a bell?

Explain Your Results

1. Draw a diagram that **communicates** how to make the machine.

Draw another diagram that **communicates** how the machine works.

2. How else could you use the machine? What else could you make with the parts?

____

____

____

Self-Assessment Checklist	
I followed instructions to set up a machine that can ring a bell.	______
I tested the machine.	______
I drew a diagram that **communicated** how to make the machine.	______
I drew another diagram that **communicated** how the machine works.	______
I reported other ways to use the machine and what else could be made with the parts.	______

Notes for Home: Your child did an activity to construct a simple machine that made a bell ring.
Home Activity: With your child, see if you can find a machine in your home that is similar to the one made in class.

Name ______________________

Use with Chapter 16, pp. 474–475

Investigate: What tasks can a machine do?

5 Make a chart. Record the task you chose, the materials and tools you used, your **prediction,** your test and the results of your test, and how you changed your device.

Task	
Design (Describe and draw your device.)	
Materials and tools used	
Prediction	
Test and test results	
Change	

Explain Your Results

1. What task did you decide to do?

____

____

2. How did you test your **prediction?**

____

____

____

3. Communicate: Explain how your change made your device work better.

____

____

____

Go Further

How would removing one part of your device affect how well it works? Demonstrate that in an object consisting of many parts, the parts usually influence or interact with one another.

____

____

Self-Assessment Checklist	
I described a task and designed and built a device made of two or more simple machines to do the task.	____
I **predicted** whether my device would do its task.	____
I **investigated** how well my device did the task and what might have caused problems.	____
I changed my device so that it would work even better and explained how the change made the device work better.	____
I explained how I tested my **prediction** and how I changed the device.	____

Notes for Home: Your child did an activity to design and build a device that can do a simple task.
Home Activity: With your child, discuss how the activity done in class is similar to the way inventors work.

Lab zone **Activity**

How can you use pulleys to change the direction of force?

Materials

What to Do

1. Put on your safety goggles. Set the block of wood on the table with the nails facing upward. Place the two large spools on the nails. Wrap a large rubber band around them as shown in the picture.

2. Turn one spool clockwise. **Observe** and record the direction in which the other spool moves.

3. Carefully turn one spool one complete turn. Record how many times the other spool turns.

4. Cross the rubber band as shown. Turn one spool clockwise. Record the direction in which the other spool moves.

5. Replace one spool with the small spool as shown. Turn the larger spool one complete turn. Record how many times the small spool moves.

6. Place the other large spool on the block and attach the spools using a second rubber band as shown. Turn the first large spool. Record how the other spools move.

7. Cross one of the rubber bands and turn the large spool. Then cross both of the rubber bands and turn the spool. Each time, record how the other spools move.

Process Skills

When you **interpret data,** you use it to answer questions.

Explain Your Results

1. **Interpreting Data** How did you change the direction of force of the pulley in this activity?
2. Name two objects that are pulleys. How are they used?

Lab zone **Activity**

How many books can you lift with your little finger?

Materials

books

pencils

What to Do

1. Place one book on the desk. Slip your little finger under the book. Try to lift the book.
2. Add another book and try to lift both books, using just your little finger. Continue adding books, one by one, until you can no longer lift the books with your little finger.
3. Place one pencil along the edge of the book stack, about 2.5 cm away. Place the unsharpened end of the other pencil under the bottom book and on top of the first pencil.
4. Using your little finger, press down on the eraser end of the second pencil and try to lift the books.
5. Move the bottom pencil farther away from the stack. Repeat step 4.
6. Repeat step 5 until the bottom pencil is near the eraser end of the top pencil.

Process Skills

Describing your observations is one way to **collect data.**

Explain Your Results

1. What type of simple machine did you **model** in this activity?
2. **Collecting Data** Describe what happened when you tried to lift the books with your finger. How did the amount of force needed to lift the books change when you used the pencil in step 4?
3. How did changing the position of the bottom pencil affect the force needed to lift the books?

Use with Chapter 16

32

Name ______________________

Use with page 31

How can you use pulleys to change the direction of force?

2. Turn one spool clockwise. **Observe** and record the direction in which the other spool moves.

____

3. Carefully turn one spool one complete turn. Record how many times the other spool turns.

____

4. Cross the rubber band as shown. Turn one spool clockwise. Record the direction in which the other spool moves.

____

5. Replace one spool with the small spool as shown. Turn the large spool one complete turn. Record how many times the small spool moves.

____

6. Place the other large spool on the block and attach the spools using a second rubber band as shown. Turn the first large spool. Record how the other spools move.

____

7. Cross one of the rubber bands and turn the large spool. Then cross both of the rubber bands and turn the spool. Each time, record how the other spools move.

____

____

____

____

Use with page 31

Explain Your Results

1. Interpret Data: How did you change the direction of force of the pulley in this activity?

____

____

2. Name two objects that are pulleys. How are they used?

____

____

Self-Assessment Checklist	
I turned one spool clockwise and **observed** how the other spool moved.	___
I crossed the rubber band and used a small spool and recorded how the spools moved each time.	___
I recorded how the spools moved when there were three spools.	___
I **interpreted my data** to explain how I changed the direction of force of the pulley.	___
I named two objects that are pulleys and described how they are used.	___

Notes for Home: Your child did an activity to **observe** how you can use pulleys to change the direction of force.
Home Activity: With your child, discuss how changing the direction of a force could be useful.

Name ______________________________

Use with page 32

How many books can you lift with your little finger?

Explain Your Results

1. What type of simple machine did you **model** in this activity?

____

2. **Collecting Data:** Describe what happened when you tried to lift the books with your finger. How did the amount of force needed to lift the books change when you used the pencil in step 4?

____

3. How did changing the position of the bottom pencil affect the force needed to lift the books?

____

____

Self-Assessment Checklist	
I followed instructions to try to lift books with my little finger.	______
I followed instructions to set up the pencils and used them to try to lift the books.	______
I **collected data** about how the amount of force needed changed when I used the pencil.	______
I named the type of simple machine that I **modeled** in this activity.	______
I explained how changing the position of the bottom pencil affected the force needed.	______

Notes for Home: Your child did an activity to **model** how a lever makes heavy objects easier to lift.
Home Activity: With your child, find and **observe** a lever somewhere in your home.

Experiment: How is motion affected by mass?

Ask a question.

How does the mass of a cup affect the distance a rolling marble will move the cup?

State a hypothesis.

If the mass of a cup is increased, then will the distance the cup is moved by a rolling marble increase, decrease, or remain the same?
Write your **hypothesis.**

____

____

Identify and control variables.

You will increase the mass of the cup by taping pennies to the cup. You will **measure** the distance the cup moves. Everything else must remain the same.

Test your hypothesis.

❶–❺ Follow the steps to perform your experiment. Record your data in the chart.

Collect and record your data.

Pennies Added	Distance Cup Moved (cm)	Mass of Cup with Pennies (g)
0		
1		
2		
3		
4		

Interpret your data.

Use your data to make a line graph.

Effect of Mass on Distance Moved

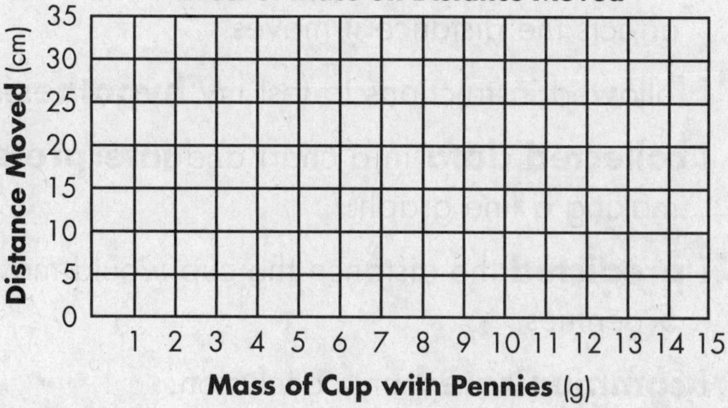

Look at your graph closely. Describe how the distance the cup moved was affected by the mass of the cup with pennies.

____

Based on the data and the pattern shown by your line graph, **predict** the distance the cup would move with 5 pennies.

____

State your conclusion.

Explain how mass affects the distance that the cup moves. Compare your hypothesis with your results. **Communicate** your conclusion.

____

____

Go Further

How would changing the height of the ramp affect how the cup moves? Design and carry out a plan to investigate this or other questions you may have. Write a procedure others can use to repeat your experiment.

____

____

Self-Assessment Checklist	
I stated my **hypothesis** about how the mass of a cup affects the distance it moves.	______
I followed instructions to test my **hypothesis.**	______
I **collected data** in a chart and **interpreted data** by making a line graph.	______
I **predicted** the distance the cup would move with 5 pennies.	______
I **communicated** my conclusion.	______

Notes for Home: Your child did an activity to determine how the mass of an object affects its motion.
Home Activity: With your child, discuss how you would test whether the mass of the marble affected the motion of the cup.

Name ______________________________

Lab zone **Directed Inquiry**

Use with Chapter 17, p. 492

Explore: What is the shape of a planet's path?

❷ **Observe** the shape carefully. Is the length from the center to the edge the same in all directions?

____

Explain Your Results

Predict the effect of moving the second pin farther from the center. How would the new shape be different?

____

____

Self-Assessment Checklist	
I followed instructions to draw a circle.	______
I followed instructions to draw an ellipse.	______
I **observed** the ellipse carefully.	______
I determined whether the length from the center to the edge was the same in all directions.	______
I **predicted** the effect of moving the second pin farther from the center.	______

Notes for Home: Your child did an activity to draw and compare an ellipse and a circle.
Home Activity: Have your child explain to you the difference between an ellipse and a circle.

Investigate: How can you make a star finder?

❺ Suppose you were going to **observe** the sky on April 1 at 9 P.M. Set the dial for 9 P.M. on April 1. **Record** the constellations you could see. Now set the dial for midnight. **Record** the constellations you could see.

Stars Visible on April 1	
Visible at 9:00 P.M.	**Visible at Midnight**

Explain Your Results

Which constellations could you **observe** at 9:00 P.M. that are not visible at midnight? Explain why.

____

____

____

Go Further

Do all stars have the same brightness, size, and color? How do stars move daily and seasonally? If possible in your area, use your star finder to help find out. Also, look for star patterns, such as the Big Dipper.

____

____

____

____

Name ______________________

Use with Chapter 17, pp. 506–507

Self-Assessment Checklist	
I followed instructions to make a star finder.	______
I practiced using the star finder in the classroom.	______
I set the dial for 9:00 P.M. on April 1 and **recorded** the constellations I could see.	______
I set the dial for midnight on April 1 and **recorded** the constellations I could see.	______
I determined which constellations I could **observe** at 9:00 P.M. that are not visible at midnight.	______

Notes for Home: Your child did an activity to make and use a Star Finder to locate constellations.
Home Activity: With your child, observe the night sky and identify 2 constellations.

Lab zone **Activity**

How can you show that the Moon rotates?

Materials

paper

marker

tape

What to Do

1. Draw a Sun on one sheet of paper. Tape the paper to the wall at eye level.
2. Draw a large circle on the second sheet of paper. Label the circle Earth.
3. Tape the "Earth" paper to the floor, about 5 feet from the wall.

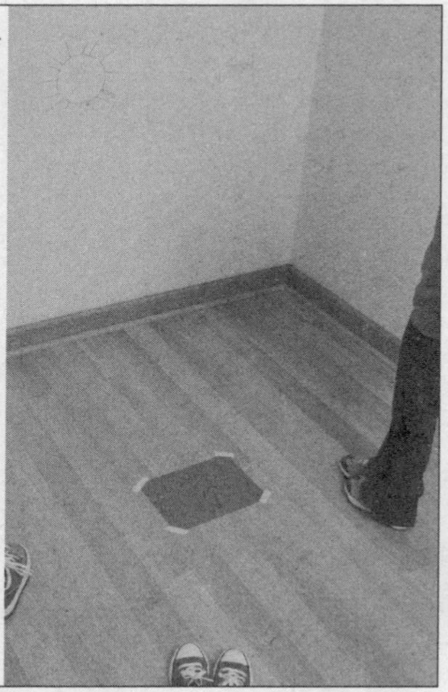

4. Stand to the right of the Earth and face the Sun on the wall.
5. Walk around the Earth, making sure that you always face the Sun.
6. Repeat steps 4 and 5. This time, however, make sure you always face the Earth as you walk around it.

Process Skills

You can **use a model** to help you understand that the Moon rotates.

Explain Your Results

1. **Use a Model** How would an observer on Earth describe your movement as you completed steps 4 and 5? Step 6?
2. How does your motion in steps 4 and 5 compare with your motion in step 6?

Use with Chapter 17

33

Lab zone Activity

Why do stars twinkle?

Materials

What to Do

1. Bunch the foil up into a medium ball. Then undo the ball and place the wrinkled foil on the table or desk.
2. Place a bowl on top of wrinkled foil. Pour water into the bowl until it is half full. Darken the room.
3. Turn on the flashlight and hold it about 30 cm above the surface of the water.

4. Observe the foil through the undisturbed water in the bowl.
5. Keep shining the light on the foil and gently tap the surface of the water with the straw.
6. Observe how the foil looks when viewed through the moving water.

Explain Your Results

1. How did the foil look when you observed it through the still water?
2. **Infer** How did the foil look when you observed it through the moving water? Explain how the observations made when the water was moving were alike and different from the observations you made when the water was calm.

Process Skills

You can **make a model** to help you understand how we see the stars.

Use with Chapter 17

34

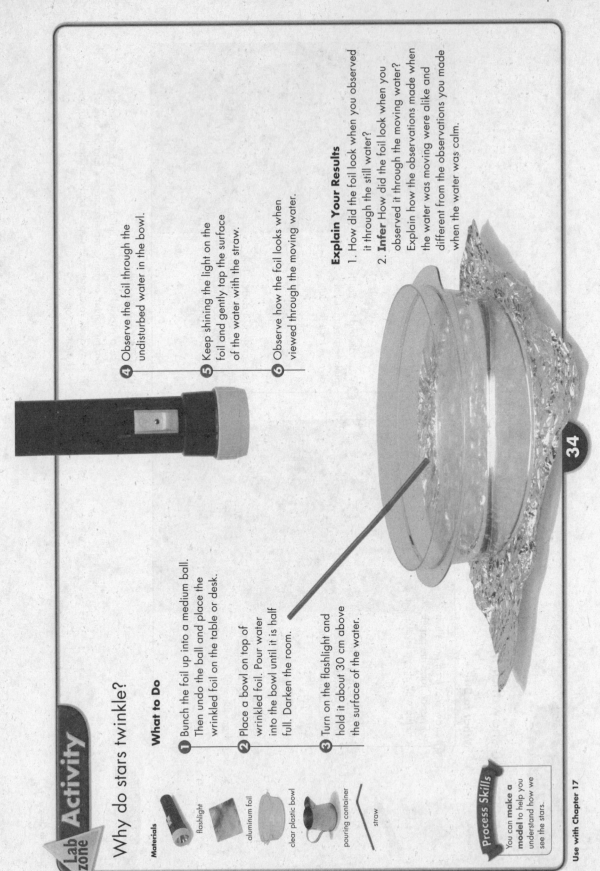

Name ______________________________

Use with page 33

How can you show that the Moon rotates?

Explain Your Results

1. **Use a Model:** How would an observer on Earth describe your movement as you completed steps 4 and 5? Step 6?

____

____

____

2. How does your motion in steps 4 and 5 compare with your motion in step 6?

____

____

____

Self-Assessment Checklist	
I drew a Sun and Earth on sheets of paper and taped them to the wall.	____
I followed instructions to walk around Earth facing the Sun.	____
I followed instructions to walk around Earth facing Earth.	____
I explained how an observer on Earth would describe the **model's** movement during each step.	____
I compared my motion in steps 4 and 5 with my motion in step 6.	____

Notes for Home: Your child did an activity to **use a model** to show that the Moon rotates.
Home Activity: With your child, discuss what causes the different phases of the Moon.

Name ______________________________

Use with page 34

Why do stars twinkle?

Explain Your Results

1. How did the foil look when you observed it through the still water?

____

2. Infer: How did the foil look when you observed it through the moving water? Explain how the observations made when the water was moving were alike and different from the observations you made when the water was calm.

____

____

____

Self-Assessment Checklist	
I followed instructions to prepare the foil and the bowl.	____
I followed instructions to turn on the flashlight and hold it 30 cm above the water.	____
I described how the foil looked when I observed it through the still water.	____
I described how the foil looked when I observed it through the moving water.	____
I made an **inference** about how the observations were alike and different.	____.

Notes for Home: Your child did an activity to **make a model** in order to understand how we see stars.
Home Activity: With your child, discuss why the stars appear to be smaller than the Sun.

Name ______________________________

Use with Chapter 18, p. 516

Explore: How can you compare the sizes of planets?

❶–❸ **Measure** the diameter of each planet. Then use your measurements and the chart to find each planet's name. Label and cut out each planet. Put the **models** of the planets in order by size. Then put the planets in order by distance from the Sun.

Name of Planet	**Diameter of Planet** (nearest 100 km)	**Diameter of Model** (mm)	**Distance from Sun** (nearest 100,000 km)
Mercury (Label with an *M*.)	4,900 km	5 mm	57,900,000 km
Venus	12,100 km	12 mm	108,200,000 km
Earth	12,800 km	13 mm	149,600,000 km
Mars	6,800 km	7 mm	227,900,000 km
Jupiter	143,000 km	143 mm	778,400,000 km
Saturn	120,500 km	121 mm	1,426,700,000 km
Uranus	51,000 km	51 mm	2,871,000,000 km
Neptune	49,500 km	50 mm	4,498,300,000 km
Pluto (Label with a *P*.)	2,300 km	2 mm	5,906,300,000 km

Explain Your Results

1. Explain how **measuring** helped you identify each paper **model**.

____

____

____

2. Compare the sizes of Earth, Venus, and Jupiter.

____

____

3. How many planets are smaller than Earth? larger than Earth?

____

____

Self-Assessment Checklist	
I measured the diameter of each planet and used my measurements and the chart to find each planet's name.	____
I first put the planets in order by size and then by distance from the Sun.	____
I explained how **measuring** helped identify each paper **model.**	____
I used the **models** to compare the size of Earth to the sizes of Venus and Jupiter.	____
I determined how many planets are smaller than Earth and how many are larger than Earth.	____

Notes for Home: Your child used **models** to compare the relative diameters of the planets of the solar system.
Home Activity: With your child, discuss why planets like Venus and Jupiter look smaller than the Moon when viewed from Earth.

Name ______________________________

Use with Chapter 18, pp. 538–539

Investigate: How does spinning affect a planet's shape?

5 Hold the pencil between your palms and move your hands back and forth to make your model spin. Record your **observations** in the chart below.

Shape When Not Spinning	Shape While Spinning
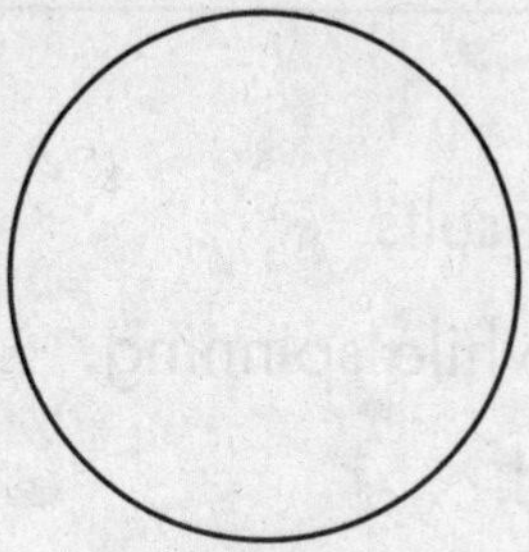 **Circle**	

Explain Your Results

1. Did the sphere change shape when you spun it? Make an **inference** about what happened.

____

____

2. How is your **model** similar to a spinning planet? How is it different?

____

____

____

Go Further

Be your own model of a spinning planet. Stand in an open area far from other students with your arms hanging loosely at your sides. Spin around twice. Feel your arms move out. Be careful not to get dizzy!

Self-Assessment Checklist	
I followed instructions to **make a model.**	______
I made my model spin and **observed** the results.	______
I drew a picture of the shape of the model while spinning.	______
I made an **inference** about what happened.	______
I determined how my model is similar to a spinning planet and how it is different.	______

Notes for Home: Your child made a model to **observe** how spinning changes the shape of the planets.
Home Activity: With your child, discuss how scientists know the Earth's rate of spin.

Lab zone **Activity**

How does a satellite stay in orbit?

Materials

What to Do

1. Make a ball of clay to use as a planet. Tie one end of the string around the clay. Roll the clay between your hands to press the string into the clay.

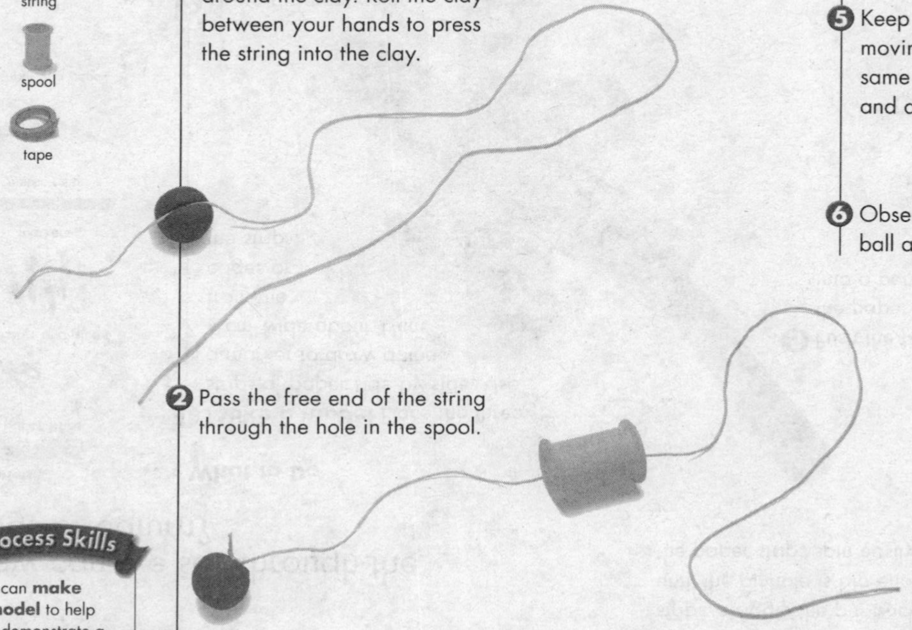

2. Pass the free end of the string through the hole in the spool.

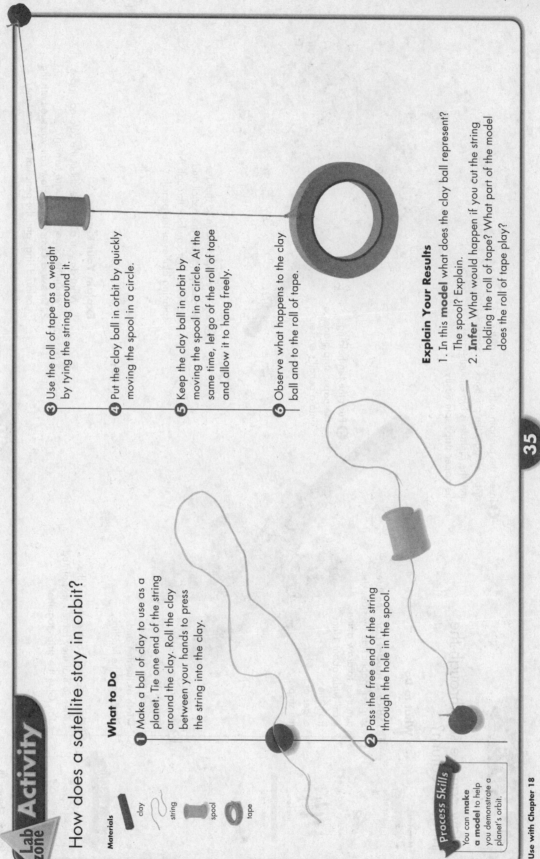

3. Use the roll of tape as a weight by tying the string around it.

4. Put the clay ball in orbit by quickly moving the spool in a circle.

5. Keep the clay ball in orbit by moving the spool in a circle. At the same time, let go of the roll of tape and allow it to hang freely.

6. Observe what happens to the clay ball and to the roll of tape.

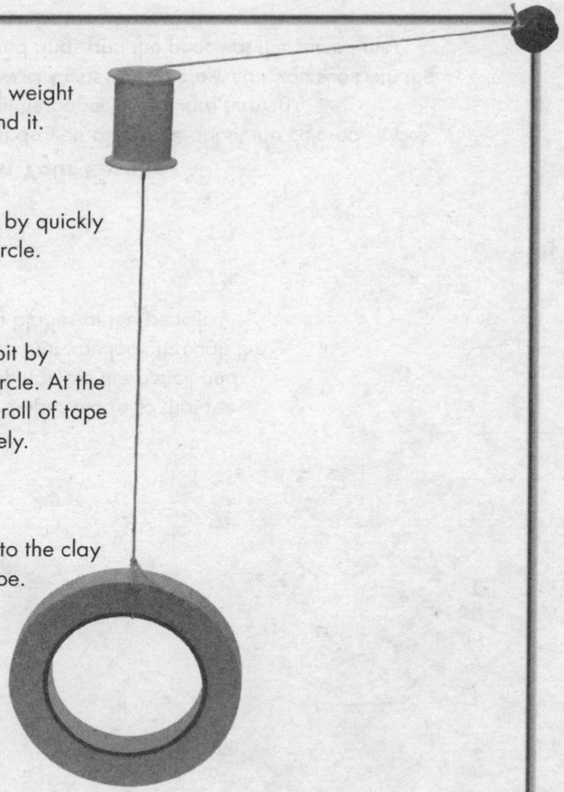

Process Skills

You can **make a model** to help you demonstrate a planet's orbit.

Explain Your Results

1. In this **model** what does the clay ball represent? The spool? Explain.
2. **Infer** What would happen if you cut the string holding the roll of tape? What part of the model does the roll of tape play?

Lab zone **Activity**

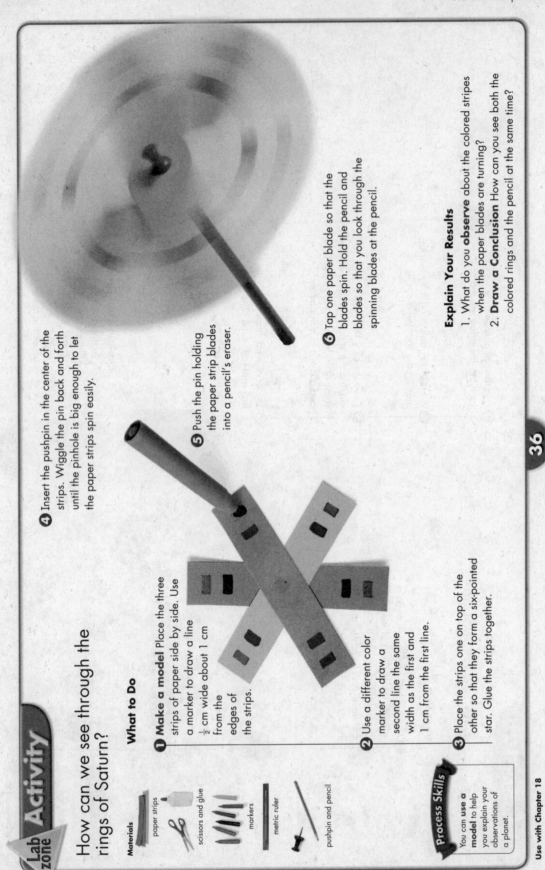

How can we see through the rings of Saturn?

Materials

What to Do

1. **Make a model** Place the three strips of paper side by side. Use a marker to draw a line $\frac{1}{2}$ cm wide about 1 cm from the edges of the strips.

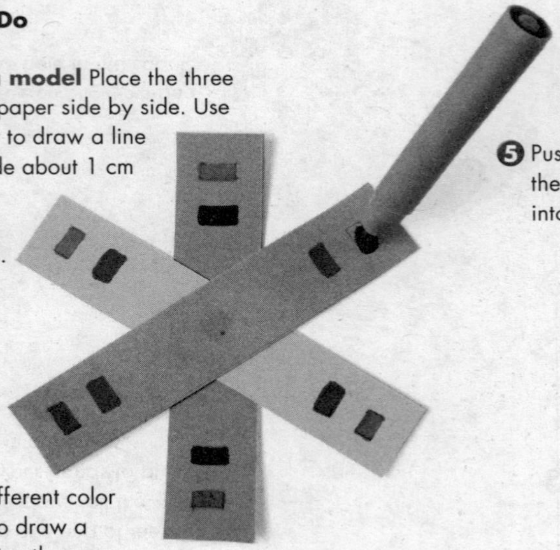

2. Use a different color marker to draw a second line the same width as the first and 1 cm from the first line.
3. Place the strips one on top of the other so that they form a six-pointed star. Glue the strips together.
4. Insert the pushpin in the center of the strips. Wiggle the pin back and forth until the pinhole is big enough to let the paper strips spin easily.
5. Push the pin holding the paper strip blades into a pencil's eraser.

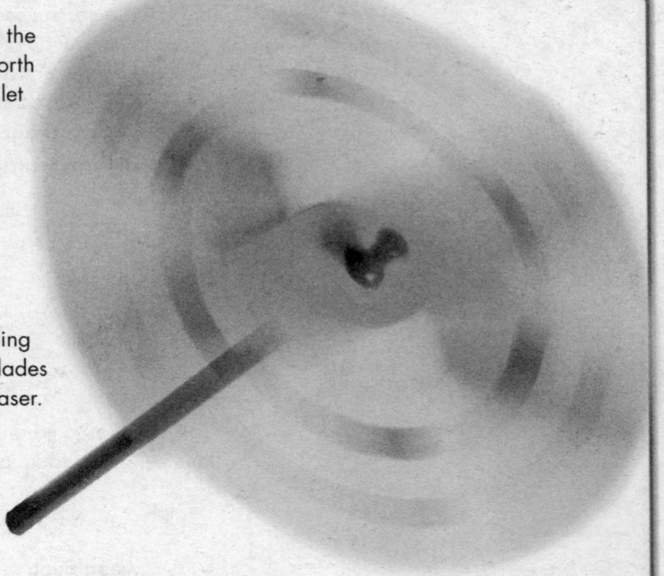

6. Tap one paper blade so that the blades spin. Hold the pencil and blades so that you look through the spinning blades at the pencil.

Process Skills

You can **use a model** to help you explain your observations of a planet.

Explain Your Results

1. What do you **observe** about the colored stripes when the paper blades are turning?
2. **Draw a Conclusion** How can you see both the colored rings and the pencil at the same time?

Use with Chapter 18

36

Name ______________________________

How does a satellite stay in orbit?

❻ Observe what happens to the clay ball and to the roll of tape.

____

Explain Your Results

1. In this model what does the clay ball represent? the spool? Explain.

____

____

2. Infer: What would happen if you cut the string holding the roll of tape? What part of the model does the roll of tape play?

____

____

____

____

Self-Assessment Checklist	
I kept the clay ball in orbit by moving the spool in a circle and let the tape hang.	____
I observed what happened to the clay ball and to the roll of tape.	____
I explained what the clay ball and the spool represent in my **model.**	____
I made an **inference** about what would happen if I cut the string holding the tape.	____
I made an **inference** about what part of the model the roll of tape played.	____

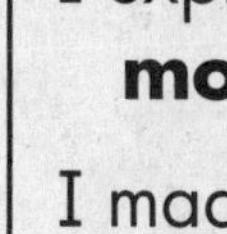

Notes for Home: Your child did an activity to **make a model** in order to demonstrate how a planet stays in orbit.
Home Activity: With your child, discuss how the orbits of the planets are elliptical and not perfect circles.

Name ______________________________

Use with page 36

How can we see through the rings of Saturn?

Explain Your Results

1. What do you **observe** about the colored stripes when the paper blades are turning?

   ____

2. **Draw a Conclusion:** How can you see both the colored rings and the pencil at the same time?

   ____

   ____

   ____

Self-Assessment Checklist	
I followed instructions to make lines on the paper and glue the strips into a star.	____
I followed instructions to attach the paper strip blades to a pencil with a pushpin.	____
I spun the blades and looked at the pencil through the spinning blades.	____
I described what I observed about the colored stripes when the paper blades were turning.	____
I **inferred** about why I could see the rings and the pencil at the same time.	____

Notes for Home: Your child did an activity to **use a model** to help explain observations about Saturn's rings.
Home Activity: With your child, discuss what kind of material makes up the rings of Saturn.

Explore: How do communications satellites work?

Explain Your Results

Infer: How do you think a communications satellite helps to send signals from place to place?

____

____

Self-Assessment Checklist	
I followed instructions to **make a model** of a communications satellite.	______
I stayed on task during this activity.	
I placed the mirror so the light from the flashlight hit the white paper.	______
I **observed** how light was reflected in my model.	______
I made an **inference** about how a communications satellite works.	______

Notes for Home: Your child **made a model** of a communications satellite.
Home Activity: Have your child explain to you how a communications satellite can be used to bring television to your home.

Name ___

Lab zone **Guided Inquiry**

Use with Chapter 19, pp. 560–561

Investigate: Why are satellite antennas curved?

5 Copy and complete the drawing. Use dotted lines to show how the light reflects off the foil.

Path of Light

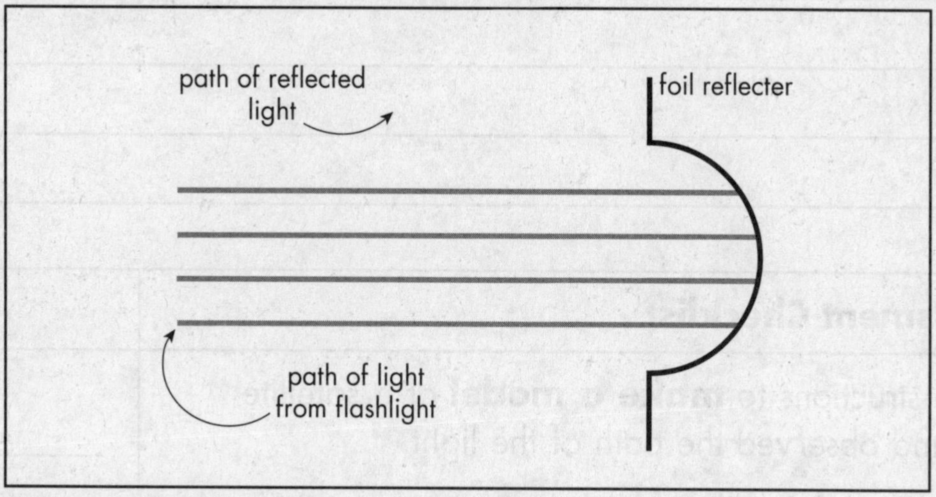

Explain Your Results

1. Infer: If a very weak signal were coming from space, would you need a large or small satellite antenna to detect it?

___

___

2. Compare and contrast your model of a satellite antenna with the real thing.

___

___

___

___

3. Explain why a satellite antenna is curved.

___

___

___

Go Further

What would be the effect of a more powerful signal or a larger antenna? Change your model to help answer this or other questions you may have.

____

____

____

____

Self-Assessment Checklist	
I followed instructions to **make a model** of a satellite antenna and observed the path of the light.	______
I copied and completed the drawing.	______
I made an **inference** about what kind of antenna would be needed to detect a weak signal.	______
I compared and contrasted my **model** of a satellite antenna with the real thing.	______
I explained why a satellite antenna is curved.	______

Notes for Home: Your child **made a model** that shows how a curved satellite antenna collects and focuses a signal.
Home Activity: Have your child explain to you how satellites can be used to send television signals.

Lab zone Activity

How strong are hook and loop fasteners?

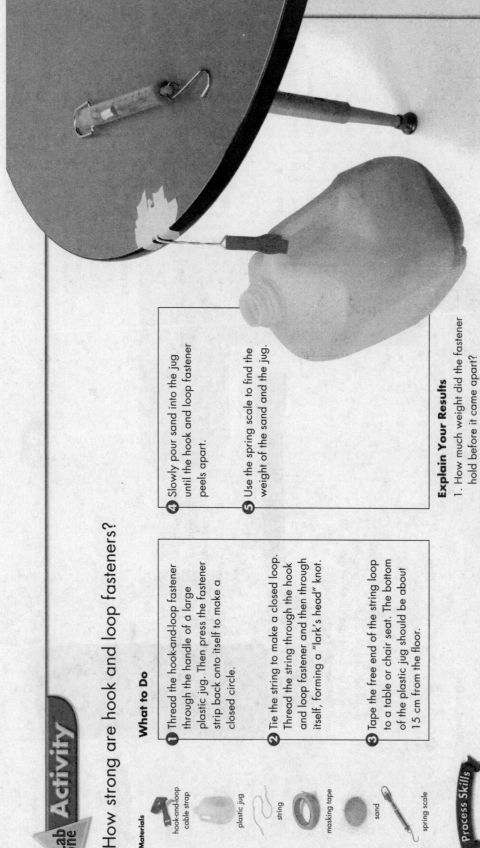

Materials

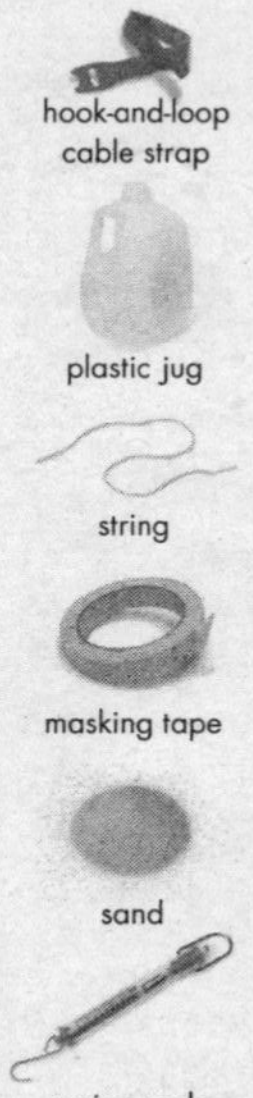

What to Do

1. Thread the hook-and-loop fastener through the handle of a large plastic jug. Then press the fastener strip back onto itself to make a closed circle.
2. Tie the string to make a closed loop. Thread the string through the hook and loop fastener and then through itself, forming a "lark's head" knot.
3. Tape the free end of the string loop to a table or chair seat. The bottom of the plastic jug should be about 15 cm from the floor.
4. Slowly pour sand into the jug until the hook and loop fastener peels apart.
5. Use the spring scale to find the weight of the sand and the jug.

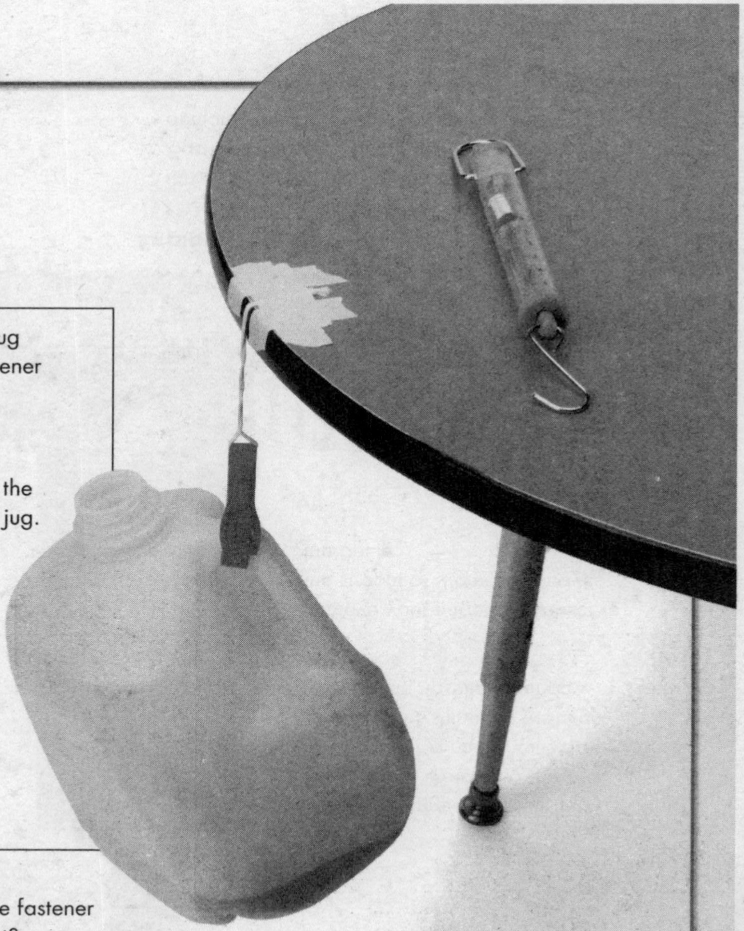

Process Skills

You can **measure** the strength of hook and loop fasteners by collecting and **interpreting data.**

Explain Your Results

1. How much weight did the fastener hold before it came apart?
2. **Infer** How would you describe the amount of weight that the hook and loop fastener could hold—small, medium, large? Explain.

Use with Chapter 19

37

Lab zone **Activity**

How can you show total internal reflection?

Materials

Process Skills

You can **make a model** to show total internal reflection of light.

What to Do

1. Cut a hole the size of the flashlight's light 3 inches from the edges of the construction paper.
2. Wrap the black paper around the bottle so that the flashlight window is near the bottom of the bottle. Do not cover the window. Tape the paper in place.

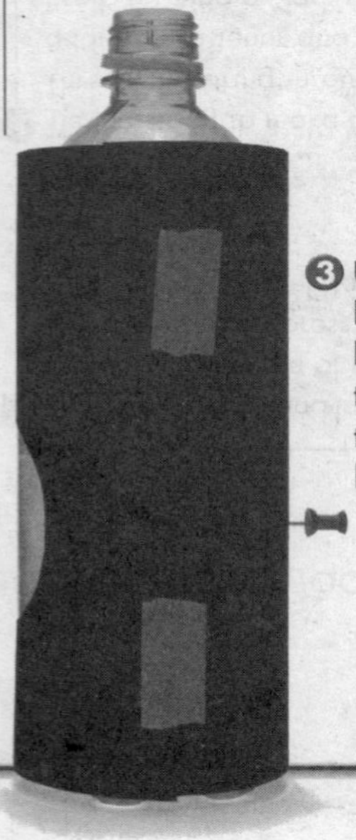

3. Use the pushpin to make a hole in the paper and the bottle. Place the hole opposite the flashlight window. Use the pushpin to make the hole larger.

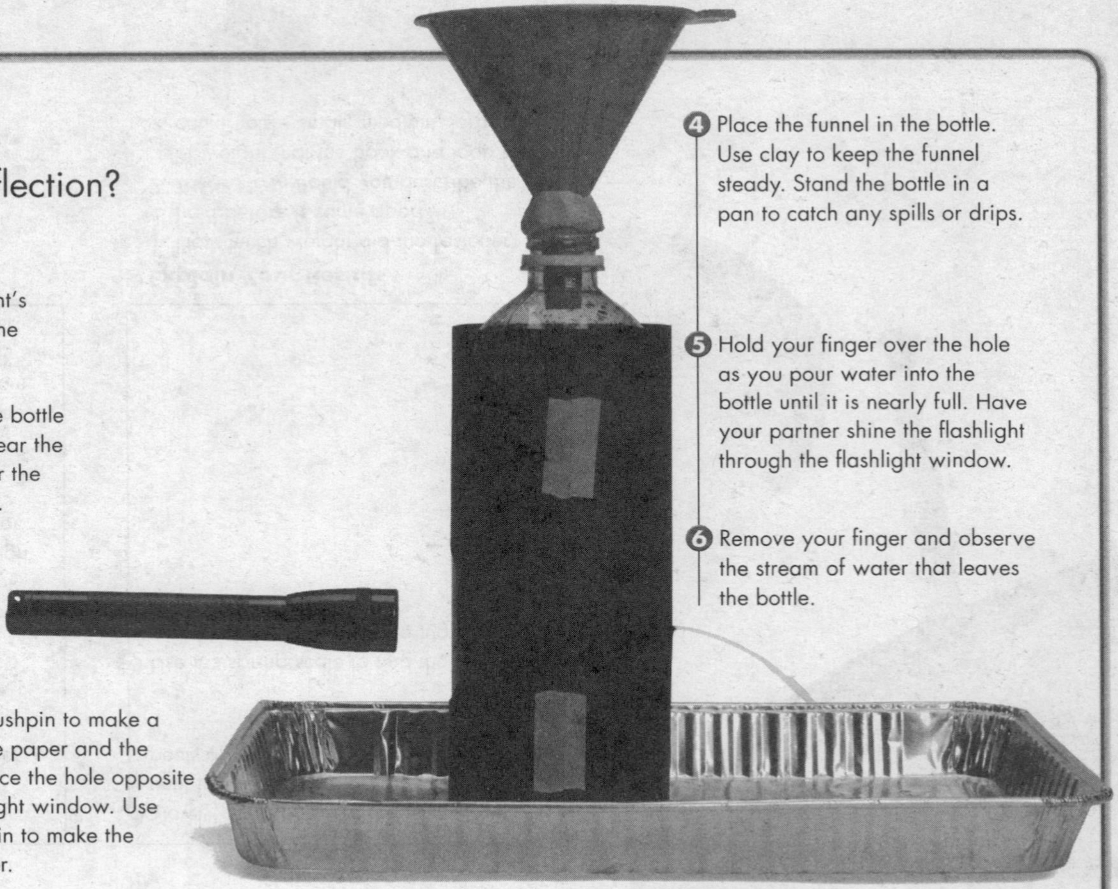

4. Place the funnel in the bottle. Use clay to keep the funnel steady. Stand the bottle in a pan to catch any spills or drips.
5. Hold your finger over the hole as you pour water into the bottle until it is nearly full. Have your partner shine the flashlight through the flashlight window.
6. Remove your finger and observe the stream of water that leaves the bottle.

Explain Your Results

1. Describe the stream of water leaving the bottle through the pinhole.
2. **Communicate** Explain how this activity demonstrates "total internal reflection" of light.

Use with Chapter 19

38

How strong are hook and loop fasteners?

Explain Your Results

1. How much weight did the fastener hold before it came apart?

____

2. Infer: How would you describe the amount of weight that the hook and loop fastener could hold—small, medium, large? Explain.

____

____

Self-Assessment Checklist	
I followed instructions to attach the fastener to the jug and hang the fastener with string.	______
I poured sand into the jug until the jug was full and the fastener peeled apart.	______
I used the spring scale to find the weight of the sand in the jug.	______
I described how much weight the fastener held before it came apart.	______
I **inferred** the amount of weight that the hook and loop fastener could hold.	______

Notes for Home: Your child did an activity to **measure** and **interpret data** about the strength of hook and loop fasteners.
Home Activity: With your child, discuss another strong material and why it is able to hold a lot of weight.

Name ______________________________

Use with page 38

How can you show total internal reflection?

Explain Your Results

1. Describe the stream of water leaving the bottle through the pinhole.

____

____

2. Communicate: Explain how this activity demonstrates "total internal reflection" of light.

____

____

____

____

Self-Assessment Checklist	
I followed instructions to prepare the bottle.	____
I followed instructions to pour the water and shine the flashlight through the flashlight window.	____
I removed my finger and observed the stream of water that left the bottle.	____
I described the stream of water leaving the bottle.	____
I **communicated** how this activity demonstrates "total internal reflection" of light.	____

Notes for Home: Your child did an activity to **make a model** to show the internal reflection of light.
Home Activity: Have your child explain to you what the internal reflection of light is.

Name ___________________________

Lab zone **Full Inquiry**

Use with Unit D, pp. 572–575

Experiment: How does payload affect the distance a model rocket can travel?

Ask a question.

How does payload affect the distance a model rocket can travel?

State a hypothesis.

____

____

Identify and control variables.

Identify the variables in your experiment.

independent variable ___________________________

dependent variable ___________________________

controlled variables ___________________________

____

Test your hypothesis.

1–8 Follow the steps to perform your experiment. Record your data in the chart.

Collect and record your data.

Payload (number of paper clips)	**Farthest Distance Rocket Traveled** (cm)
0	
2	
4	

Name ________________________________

Full Inquiry

Use with Unit D, pp. 572–575

Interpret your data.

On a separate sheet of paper, use your data to make a bar graph. Analyze how the number of paper clips carried by your rocket affected the distance it traveled. Explain your results.

____

____

____

State your conclusion.

Compare your hypothesis with your results. **Communicate** your conclusion.

____

____

Go Further

How would adding fins affect how far the rocket travels? In your science journal, write and carry out a plan to investigate.

Self-Assessment Checklist	
I stated my **hypothesis** about how increasing the payload would affect the distance the rocket traveled.	______
I followed instructions to test my **hypothesis** and **measured** the results.	______
I **collected data** in a chart about how far the rocket traveled with different payloads.	______
I **interpreted my data** to explain how the payload affected the distance traveled.	______
I **communicated** my conclusion about how the payload affected the distance my rocket traveled.	______

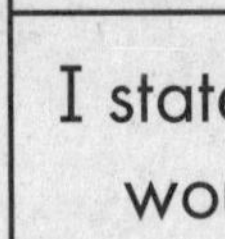

Notes for Home: Your child did an activity to **measure** how the payload affects the distance a model rocket can travel.
Home Activity: Have your child explain to you 2 ways that a rocket with a heavier payload could travel the same distance as a rocket with a lighter payload.